now
and
not
yet

DISCOVERING SIX WAYS GOD IS MORE
FAITHFUL THAN YOU KNOW

BIBLE STUDY GUIDE + STREAMING VIDEO
SIX SESSIONS

RUTH CHOU SIMONS

HarperChristian
Resources

Now and Not Yet Bible Study Guide

© 2024 by Ruth Chou Simons

Published in Grand Rapids, Michigan, by HarperChristian Resources. HarperChristian Resources is a registered trademark of HarperCollins Christian Publishing, Inc.

Requests for information should be sent to customercare@harpercollins.com.

ISBN 978-0-310-16189-9 (softcover)
ISBN 978-0-310-16190-5 (ebook)

All Scripture quotations are taken from the ESV® Bible (The Holy Bible, English Standard Version®). Copyright © 2001 by Crossway, a publishing ministry of Good News Publishers. Used by permission. All rights reserved.

Any internet addresses (websites, blogs, etc.) and telephone numbers in this study guide are offered as a resource. They are not intended in any way to be or imply an endorsement by HarperChristian Resources, nor does HarperChristian Resources vouch for the content of these sites and numbers for the life of this study guide.

All rights reserved. No portion of this book may be reproduced, stored in a retrieval system, or transmitted in any form or by any means—electronic, mechanical, photocopy, recording, scanning, or other—except for brief quotations in critical reviews or articles, without the prior written permission of the publisher.

HarperChristian Resources titles may be purchased in bulk for church, business, fundraising, or ministry use. For information, please e-mail ResourceSpecialist@ChurchSource.com.

First Printing June 2024 / Printed in the United States of America

Contents

Session Four: God Hears Your Cries

Session 5: God's Sufficiency Meets Your Weakness

Session Six: God's Sanctifying Work Is Sure

A Note from Ruth

Dear friend,

I may not know what kind of season you're in as you enter into this study . . . *Is it heavy? Are you doing okay or struggling?* I don't know why you're doing this Bible study . . . *Did you choose it yourself or are you just along for the ride?* And, I don't know what you're anticipating . . . *Are you excited? Hopeful? Reluctant?*

But here's one thing I do know: I'm so glad you're here.

I've started Bible studies in every way that I just listed: on purpose, accidentally, excitedly, reluctantly, hurting, and happy. And no matter how I came, God has faithfully met me in His Word. So, I'm confidently praying He does the same for you regardless of your circumstance or season.

This Bible study is for anyone who has ever wished they were somewhere else, further along, or done with their present circumstance. It's for the woman who has wondered if God truly sees her and whether He really cares. It's for those of us who have doubted His trustworthiness and questioned His faithfulness in our now, while waiting for all that is yet to come.

Friend, this study is for me just as much as it's for you.

As I've thought, written, and spoken about the faithfulness of God that we're about to explore, my own heart has been strengthened and encouraged. Because He really is *more faithful* than we know . . . He's more faithful than we can grasp with our finite minds, and His faithfulness is deeper and broader than it might appear on the surface. His faithfulness is on every page and in every story, and I can't wait to dive into it with you.

Because of grace,

Ruth

How to Use This Bible Study

Each week of this study is split into two sections—first up is the group session where you watch the teaching video as an introduction to the week. The second section is personal study, which includes five days of homework designed to help you unpack the theme on your own after watching the video.

GROUP SESSION STRUCTURE AND FLOW

The *Now and Not Yet* video curriculum is designed to be experienced in a group setting such as a Bible study or small group or used to help guide a weekend retreat. After watching each video session, you and the members of your group will participate in a time of discussion and reflection on what you've learned. If you have a larger group (more than twelve people), consider breaking up into smaller groups during the discussion time. For the group time each week, I invite you to start by reading a quick opening thought along with a short Scripture passage that will be discussed in the video. There's a warm-up question to help you start thinking about what you'll be discussing for the session, too. Depending on your group dynamics, you can have a couple of people share their answers or let it serve as more of a rhetorical question.

As you watch the teaching video together, feel free to take notes or just listen. After the video, you'll use the discussion questions to help process what you've heard. You may or may not talk about every question, and that's okay.

You can also do this study solo and reap the benefits. I encourage you to take the time to engage with the discussion questions and consider sharing your insights, revelations, or thoughts with a friend or family member.

MATERIALS AND FACILITATION

Each participant should have their own study guide, which includes video outline notes, group discussion questions, and a personal study section to deepen learning between sessions. Each study guide comes with individual streaming video access (instructions found on the inside front cover). Every member of your group has full access to watch videos from the convenience of their chosen devices at any time—for missed group meetings, for rewatching, for sharing teaching with others, or for watching videos individually and then meeting if your group is short on meeting time and that makes the group experience doable and more realistic.

Each group should appoint a facilitator who is responsible for starting the video and keeping track of time during the activities and discussion. Facilitators may also read questions aloud, monitor discussions, prompt participants to respond, and ensure everyone has the opportunity to participate.

Lastly, I've written a short prayer to help close out your time. Feel free to read it out loud or simply use it as a springboard for your own prayer.

PERSONAL STUDY

Each week, you'll find five days of homework, but feel free to progress through the content at whatever pace works best for you.

You'll notice that I'm encouraging you to begin and end every day of study with **prayer**. The beginning prayer is always the same: that God will teach you from His Word and that the Holy Spirit will help you apply that truth to your life. I want to start this way because without God's help, we'll just read words and answer questions. But *with* His help, God can use this study to transform our hearts.

The short prayer at the end of each day represents what I'm praying over you and alongside you. Day 5 prayers are liturgies I specifically wrote for *Now and Not Yet,* and I hope they encourage you and give voice to what you're wrestling through in the not-yet-wonderful seasons you may be facing.

Here's what else you can expect from each week:

- **Day 1**: Because the Bible is primarily a story about God, and this study is an exploration of His faithfulness, we'll begin each week with a brief overview of a specific characteristic of God.
- **Day 2**: This is a heavy-lifting day where we'll do *a lot* of reading and observing of that week's biblical character. We'll look at the big picture of the character's life, so we have context for the rest of the week's study. As you read and observe, remember: these are *real* people with *real* lives who interact with a *real* God. Because this day tends to have longer passages to read, feel free to split it up over a couple of days if that serves you well.
- **Day 3:** At this point in the week, we'll look for the intersection of days 1 and 2; the ways we see God's character on display in the person's life, and how it points to God's faithfulness.
- **Day 4**: On day 4, we'll look to the biblical character as an example or pattern for how we can respond to God in the not-yet-wonderful seasons of our own lives—tangible ways to exercise our trust in His faithfulness.
- **Day 5**: At the end of each week's study, we'll spend time reflecting on all we've taken in. It may be tempting to skip this day of study or just scribble a few quick thoughts down to say you've done it, but I encourage you to engage with the questions thoughtfully. If we never pause to meditate on the Word and think about how it applies to our lives and, yes, actually write it down, what change can we expect?

So, gather your people, call a friend, and commit to this six-week journey together. I'm cheering you on and praying for your encouragement!

God Keeps His Promises

GROUP SESSION

OPENING

Have a volunteer read the opening out loud for the group.

Whether it's a story about a promise kept or a promise broken, and whether you were on the giving or receiving end, chances are high that you have a story or memory tied to a specific promise that was made. Maybe it's something from your childhood, or maybe it's much more recent. Perhaps it brings you much joy to recall . . . or maybe it's incredibly painful.

Either way, it's clear that promises *mean* something. And they're often connected with strong emotions. Maybe, more than anything, every promise we've ever made, kept, or broken highlights a deep longing . . . we *want* every promise to be kept! We long for someone trustworthy enough to make a promise and deliver on it without fail. As hard as we might try to be that person, there's truly only One trustworthy enough: God Himself.

For the next six weeks, we're discovering some of the ways that God is more faithful than we know. May this truth and the stories we explore encourage us to trust Him more and more.

SCRIPTURE: GENESIS 15:1–6

Open your Bibles and have a volunteer read this week's Scripture out loud for the group. It doesn't matter which translation you have—reading God's Word together is always a good idea!

WARM-UP QUESTION

Take a few moments to think about the question individually before asking for one or two volunteers to share their answers with the group.

Have you ever been given a task you didn't feel equipped to accomplish? How did you feel? What was the result?

WATCH THE SESSION ONE VIDEO

Scripture referenced in this session: Genesis 12:1–4, 15; 17:19–21; Hebrews 11:8; Numbers 23:19; Psalm 36:5; 2 Thessalonians 3:3

Feel free to use this space to take notes.

GROUP DISCUSSION QUESTIONS

Use the following questions to help process the themes from the video session. You may not get to every question and that's okay!

(If you are doing this study solo, don't miss the opportunity to engage with these questions and personal prayer time.)

1. Do you have any firsthand experience of God's faithfulness that you're willing to share with the group?

2. Does your current season feel like a not-yet-wonderful one? In what ways?

3. Are you naturally inclined to believe that God is faithful, or more inclined to doubt His faithfulness? Why?

4. What stood out to you from Ruth's teaching about the covenant God made with Abraham? (If you have time, read the passages related to the covenant together in Genesis 12:1–3, Genesis 15:9–21, and Genesis 17:6–7.)

5. Are there any other verses or passages that come to mind when you think about the faithfulness of God?

PRAY

Spend some time praying together before dismissing the group.

Lord, thank You for bringing this specific group of people together for this specific study at this specific time. We need Your Holy Spirit to help us make connections we won't make on our own. So, as we read and study and discuss, open our eyes to Your faithfulness in the biblical stories we study and in our own lives. We ask this in the name of Jesus, amen.

HOMEWORK

Set aside time this week to work through the personal study on the following pages. The personal study will unpack themes from today's teaching and help you delve deeper into God's Word. Do as much as you can to get the full benefit!

God Keeps His Promises

PERSONAL STUDY

SESSION ONE OBJECTIVES:

- See what the Bible says about God's faithfulness as a promise-keeper.
- Explore the story of Abraham to see an example of God's faithfulness.
- See God's faithfulness on display in the covenant He makes with Abraham.
- Explore how we can respond to God's faithfulness, even when it feels impossible, by believing what God says.

This week's study draws on themes from chapter 7 of *Now and Not Yet*.

Day 1 | God Is Faithful

Before you begin today's study, take a moment to quiet your mind and pray. Ask God to teach you from His Word, and ask the Holy Spirit to help you apply that truth to your life.

> "The Rock, his work is perfect, for all his ways are justice. A God of faithfulness and without iniquity, just and upright is he."
> Deuteronomy 32:4

Have you ever made a promise you couldn't keep, or been on the receiving end of a broken promise?

There's something inside each of us that longs for someone to "believe in," isn't there? An ache for someone so steady, so unmovable, so trustworthy, that we can always believe what they say. No hesitation. No holding back. Just believing, with full confidence, that what they say is what they mean, and what they promise is what they'll do.

Webster's dictionary defines a promise as: "a declaration that one will do or refrain from doing something specified; a reason to expect something."[1] When you consider this definition, it's clear that the strength of the promise is in the character of the promise-maker. If a highly untrustworthy individual promises to take care of an important task, you're less likely to turn that task over, right?

Today, we're going to investigate some of the biblical evidence of the faithfulness of God. When we remember how faithful He is, we can rest assured that He really will do what He says He will do . . . that He always keeps His promises.

God's faithfulness means that He will always do what He has said and fulfill what He has promised.[2] He has never failed to keep any of His promises.[3]

Read each of the following passages and write down what you learn about the faithfulness of God.

READ	OBSERVATIONS ABOUT GOD'S FAITHFULNESS
Numbers 23:19	
2 Samuel 7:27–28	
Exodus 34:6–7	
Joshua 23:14	
2 Timothy 2:11–13	
Psalm 36:5	
1 John 1:9	
Titus 1:1–3	

I hope these passages help settle the truth deep in your heart: God *is* faithful. He *is* trustworthy.

THE PROMISES OF GOD

Now that we've seen how the Bible describes the faithfulness of God, let's turn our attention to some of the specific promises of God. If you've been a follower of Jesus for very long, several promises of God likely come to mind as we enter into this week's study. Make a list of any promises that come to mind right away:

BIBLE FACTS

One researcher estimated that there are more than 8,000 promises made in the Bible and roughly 7,400 of them are promises made by God to humankind.[4]

———

More than 300 prophecies about the coming Messiah were fulfilled in the birth, life, death, and resurrection of Jesus.[5] The statistical probability of that being true is astronomical . . . and yet *not* for God.

Consider how many of the promises you listed have been fully realized at this point in your life. All of them? None of them? Some of them?

Welcome to the real tension of "now and not yet," friend! We'll dig into this reality more as we continue this study, but for now, suffice it to say that there are many promises of God where we've only experienced partial fulfillment. And, some that we have yet to partake in the fulfillment of at all.

Regardless of how many promises we've seen the fulfillment of, one thing is sure: God makes promises that He *will* keep.

You might be surprised to find that the word *promise* only appears thirty times in the ESV Old Testament. It seems like it should be much higher, right? Ironically, there's no word in the Hebrew language that corresponds to *promise*. Instead, we find *speak*, *say*, and *word* used to describe the weight of

God's message (promises) to His people. As one writer put it, "God's word itself is the same as a promise."[6]

Let's look at just a few of the Old Testament promises made and see what we can observe.

BIBLE FACTS

Hebrew is the language Old Testament Scripture was originally written in.

READ	PROMISE (WHAT IS THE PROMISE AND WHO IS IT MADE TO?)	PROMISE FULFILLED?
Genesis 3:14–15		
Joshua 21:43–45		
1 Kings 8:55–56		
1 Kings 17:13–16		

Take a moment to record any observations you have about this list of promises. Are there any similarities that stand out to you? Any anomalies?

Friend, today we've only scratched the surface of what God's Word tells us about His faithfulness and the promises He makes, but I hope you take to heart what you've seen evidence of:

God is trustworthy. God is faithful. He keeps His promises.

GETTING PERSONAL

Each week, at the end of Days 1–4, we'll take a step back and make some connections to our own lives. This reflection step is designed to help you think deeply and start applying the truth you've read or studied . . . so don't skip it!

On a scale of 1 (not at all confident) to 10 (totally confident), how confident are you that God is faithful or trustworthy? What personal evidence (in either direction) comes to mind?

1	2	3	4	5	6	7	8	9	10

NOT AT ALL CONFIDENT   **TOTALLY CONFIDENT**

What promises of God are you holding on to in your current season?

CLOSING PRAYER

Lord, we echo the father in Mark 9:24: "I believe; help my unbelief!" Your Word tells us You are trustworthy, and we want to wholeheartedly believe it, in our minds and in our actions. Help us see Your trustworthiness on display in our own lives and believe that You keep Your promises, not only on an intellectual level but on a tangible, emotional level, too. In Jesus' name, we pray, amen.

Day 2 | Abram's Story: An Unlikely Father

Before you begin today's study, take a moment to quiet your mind and pray. Ask God to teach you from His Word, and ask the Holy Spirit to help you apply that truth to your life.

Today, we're digging into Abram's story to observe the faithfulness of God. As we'll see later this week, Abram's faith is referred to several times in the New Testament—it's worth a close look!

We won't cover the entire narrative of his life, but we will read a large chunk of it. As you read, look for ways you see his faith in God through both his actions and words.

Persevere in your reading and observing today, friend!

1. The Initial Call of Abram

Read Genesis 12:1–9. What is it that the Lord asks Abram to do?

What does the Lord promise to Abram? (verses 1–3)

A NOTE
Each week, we'll look at a narrative to gain perspective and see a tangible example of the faithfulness of God. It's helpful to keep in mind that this means each narrative is descriptive, and not necessarily prescriptive.

STUDY TIP
Remember, the second day of each week's study is designed to help you see a big-picture story of one person's life. In order to get a big picture, we'll primarily be reading (a lot of!) Scripture and making observations. This context is what we'll draw on for the rest of the week, so take your time and feel free to split up today's study over more than one day if that serves you well.

What is Abram's response to the Lord's instruction?

In verse 4:

In verses 7 and 8:

2. God's Covenant with Abram

Read Genesis 15:1–21. What is Abram's question to God in verses 2–3?

What is God's answer in verses 4–5?

What is Abram's response to God's answer in verse 6?

3. Sarai's Great Idea

Go back to Genesis 11:30. What's the very first thing we learn about Sarai?

Now, read Genesis 16:1–6. Summarize what happens in this passage.

How long does verse 3 tell us Abram and Sarai have waited up to this point?

How old is Abram at this point (Genesis 16:16)?

4. Covenant Requirements of Abram

Read Genesis 17:1–27. How old is Abram now?

What happens in verse 5?

What promises does God repeat in verses 6–8?

Summarize what God asks Abraham to do as a sign of the covenant.

Summarize Abraham's response to God's instruction in verses 22–27.

5. The Birth of Isaac

Read Genesis 21:1–8. How old is Abraham when Isaac is born?

Look back at Genesis 12:4. How many years have passed since God called Abraham to follow Him?

6. The Test

Read Genesis 22:1–24. What does God ask Abraham to do with Isaac?

What's Abraham's response to God's instruction in verse 3?

In verse 5, how does Abraham describe what he's going to do to the men accompanying him?

BIBLE FACT

Abram means "exalted father" and Abraham means "father of a multitude."[1]

Summarize what happens on the mountain.

DIG DEEPER

Other Name Changes in Scripture:

Jacob | Genesis 32:22–32

Daniel | 1:1–7

Simon | John 1:25–42

Take a moment to reflect on the parts of Abraham's life we read about today. What stands out to you about Abraham? What surprises you? What's something you may not have noticed before?

How would you summarize Abraham's "not yet"?

The time you spent in Abraham's story sets us up for the rest of this week's story—thank you for the time you invested!

GETTING PERSONAL

What part(s) of Abraham's story, if any, resonates with your own experience?

While Abraham waited, he took steps of faith:

- He followed God's instructions instead of forming his own plan.
- He expected God to provide.
- He didn't wait to receive God's provision before he obeyed.
- He trusted God's wisdom instead of his own.

What steps of faith might you need to take while you wait?

While you navigate the "not yet" circumstances of your life, consider which truths are most difficult for you to believe:

- What God says about who He is and His character
- What God says about who you are
- What God says about how to live as a follower of Jesus

CLOSING PRAYER

God, thank You for giving us a look into the life of Abraham in Your Word! Thank You for all the ways we see him trust You and continue to obey, even when what You've promised feels entirely unlikely. Help us confidently trust and obey You in the midst of our not-yet seasons, too. In Jesus' name, amen.

Day 3 | God's Faithfulness
on Display: Covenant

Before you begin today's study, take a moment to quiet your mind and pray. Ask God to teach you from His Word, and ask the Holy Spirit to help you apply that truth to your life.

Today, we're doing a deep dive into the covenant God made with Abram because it puts God's faithfulness on display in powerful ways. I can't wait for you to see it!

Turn back to Genesis 15 and read verses 7–21.

What questions does Abraham ask in verse 8?

I love that the Bible records this question for us because it's surely the question that would have been on the tip of my tongue, too: "Lord, how do I know what You're saying is for real?!" It was hard to imagine God's promise coming to fruition: Abram was childless. He had no deed or contract for the land God told him he'd possess. He wanted assurance, so he asked God for it. And God gives it to him!

COVENANTS

In its simplest definition, a covenant is described as a contract between two or more parties. However, as Kevin DeYoung points out, "Covenants in the Bible, however, are about more than contracts. They are about people. A covenant is a commitment that establishes a relationship between two or more persons."[1]

We have a record of several covenants in the Bible, and this one with Abram is central to the overarching arc of redemption.

So, while God's response to Abraham's question may seem bizarre from a modern Western perspective, the ceremony that takes place was very familiar to the original Old Testament readers.

Let's make some basic observations from Genesis 15:7–21.

What does God ask Abraham to bring?

What does Abraham do with the animals?

Are you thinking, "What in the *world*?!" yet? You're not alone! Here's a bit of historical cultural background for context:

"In our day a contract often becomes legally binding when the parties sign a document detailing the terms of the agreement. In a similar way, ancient covenants often became binding by killing and cutting an animal. This may sound foreign to us in modern society, but the phrases 'cut a deal' and 'strike a bargain' appear to have come into English from the wording of ancient covenant-making practices involving animal slaughter." [3]

CONTEXT
The "arc of redemption" refers to the big-picture story of God and His relationship to humanity as described in the Bible. It's generally characterized by four specific plot movements: Creation, Fall, Redemption, and New Creation.[2]

CONTEXT
For additional context, read a parallel narrative in Jeremiah 34:8-22 about a covenant established between Zedekiah and the people of Judah.

DIG DEEPER
Read more examples of God's presence appearing as fire:

Exodus 13:21-22

Psalm 29:1-7

Psalm 50:1-3

A *typical* ancient Near Eastern covenant would have involved promises being made by both a superior party (the suzerain) and an inferior party (the vassal). During the ceremony, each one of them would verbalize their individual responsibilities per the terms of the covenant. In general, the vassal's list of responsibilities would be much longer than the suzerain. The vassal would cut animals in half and to complete the ceremony, he'd walk between the pieces in a symbolic demonstration of what would happen to him if he broke the covenant.[4]

But, as we'll see, the Lord's covenant with Abraham is anything but typical!

The Bible tells us that as the sun goes down, God causes Abraham to fall into a deep sleep. Wait, what about the promises Abraham is supposed to make to God during the ceremony? How will he make them in his sleep? He's supposed to walk between the torn pieces of animal flesh!

But that's not what happens.

With so much at stake and such a significant promise, God chose to put Abraham to sleep while He completed the ceremony *by Himself.*

Read verse 17 and fill in the blanks:

". . . a _____ and a _____ passed between these pieces."

What does fire symbolize in this ceremony? The presence of God Himself!

God passes through the pieces of the animals, takes *all* of the responsibility, and formalizes the promises He's already made to Abraham.

God put Abraham to sleep to prove a point: Abraham had *no* part in securing the promise.

This was God's grace on display: unmerited favor, kindness, mercy, and complete provision. And nothing about this display was dependent on Abraham—not on what he did, what he said, or how he responded. He slept and God made the covenant. *God's* faithfulness was the guarantee for the promise.

What response or emotions do you have based on this picture of God's faithfulness?

MORE FAITHFUL THAN YOU KNOW: THE NEW COVENANT

Friend, the best part about this covenant with Abraham points us to something *even better!*

In the same way that God walked through animal halves to make a covenant with Abraham, He established a new covenant through the broken and bloody body of Jesus.

God's promise to forgive our sins because of the righteous life, death, and resurrection of Jesus Christ is a covenant based on what Christ alone has done—it has nothing to do with our ability or a promise we've made. Again, *God's* faithfulness guaranteed the promise.

Read 2 Corinthians 1:20 and write it out below.

The faithfulness of God that we see in Abraham's story never changes! And in Jesus, every promise God has made is "Yes."

One Old Testament professor, summarizing a framework described by John Piper,[5] describes how the promises made to Abraham are also ours:[6]

Ultimately, the faithfulness of God on display in the life of Abraham points us to the faithfulness of God on display in the life of *everyone* who follows Jesus.

What synonyms or words other than "faithful" come to mind when describing God after today's study?

Friend, I hope you're beginning to see it: He really is more faithful than we know!

GETTING PERSONAL

Have you ever asked a question of the Lord as Abraham did: "How am I to know that I shall possess it?" (Genesis 15:8). What question were you asking?

What emotions were running through your heart?

Did God respond? If so, how?

In what ways can you see His faithfulness on display, either in His immediate response or retrospectively?

CLOSING PRAYER

Lord, Great is Your faithfulness! It's too big and too wonderful for us to wrap our minds all the way around, but what we do understand is Your kindness to us. Thank You for sending Jesus. Thank You for fulfilling every promise in Him—whether we see it now or wait for fulfillment upon His return. You are more faithful than we know, and we are grateful recipients of Your grace. Remind us when we forget— You are trustworthy. In Jesus' name, we pray, amen.

Day 4 | Believe What God Says Is True

Before you begin today's study, take a moment to quiet your mind and pray. Ask God to teach you from His Word, and ask the Holy Spirit to help you apply that truth to your life.

Now that we've traced the contours of God's character (He is trustworthy and faithful!), Abraham's backstory, and God's covenant with him, we're going to spend some time considering what Abraham's example is for us, *today*.

What is it that we can take away from the way Abraham responded to God?

ABRAHAM'S EXAMPLE

Using your notes and observations from day 2, remind yourself how Abraham responded to God in each of the following parts of his story.

	WHAT DID GOD ASK ABRAHAM TO DO?	HOW DID ABRAHAM RESPOND?
The Initial Call of Abraham Genesis 12:1–9		
God's Covenant with Abraham Genesis 15:1–21		

	WHAT DID GOD ASK ABRAHAM TO DO?	HOW DID ABRAHAM RESPOND?
Failure with Hagar Genesis 16:1–16		
Covenant Requirements Genesis 17:1–27		
Birth of Isaac Genesis 21:1–21		
The Test Genesis 22:1–24		

What words or phrases come to mind to summarize Abraham's general posture toward God?

Do you see any habits or regular rhythms in his life that might have helped cultivate that posture?

What words or phrases come to mind to summarize your current posture toward God?

What habits or regular rhythms in your life are (for better or for worse) cultivating your current posture toward God?

ABRAHAM IN THE NEW TESTAMENT

What's both encouraging and challenging about Abraham's example is that it's so very *ordinary*. What God does for him is *extraordinary*, but Abraham's consistent response is one of quiet belief . . . trusting God, and taking Him at His word, over and over again.

There are lots of vignettes from Abraham's life and faith referred to in the New Testament by more than one author, but let's take a look at three specific categories that show up.

Read each passage and write down your observations about Abraham's faith.

READ	WHO OR WHAT IS ABRAHAM BELIEVING IN?
Romans 4:3	
Galatians 3:5–7	
James 2:22–23	
Romans 4:16–21	
Hebrews 11:17–19	

In case there's any question, yes, Abraham's ordinary response is that **he believed God.** Day in and day out. When it felt like the promise would never be fulfilled and when God asked for what had to have felt like an impossible request. When the only response Sarah could give was laughter, and when Abraham told the men he was going to worship. He simply believed that what God said was true.

"Indeed, the essence of true faith is taking God at his word and relying on him to do as he has promised."[1]

It's not hard to see the life of Abraham in this quote, but don't miss how it applies to you and me right now.

Saving faith in Jesus Christ requires that we believe what God, in His Word, says is true:

"For 'everyone who calls on the name of the Lord will be saved.'" Romans 10:13

"Therefore, if anyone is in Christ, he is a new creation. The old has passed away; behold, the new has come." 2 Corinthians 5:17

"For our sake he made him to be sin who knew no sin, so that in him we might become the righteousness of God." 2 Corinthians 5:21

But believing what God says is true extends beyond saving faith, too. The Bible lays out clear instructions for how God's people are to live—how to conduct ourselves, the structure of a family, how the body of Christ interacts . . . even guidelines for something as personal as sexuality. In each aspect of life, when the rubber meets the road, the question is the same:

Will you believe what God says is true?

Even when it's hard? When what He's promised seems impossible? When what He's asking you to do is counterintuitive to your own sensibility?

Friend, God *is* faithful. He *always* keeps His promises. You *can* believe what He says is true.

Will you?

GETTING PERSONAL

What part(s) of Abraham's example encourages you the most?

What part(s) of Abraham's example challenges you the most?

In what areas of your life do you find it difficult to believe God or take Him at His word?

What habits, rhythms, or practices might help you cultivate ordinary faith or trust in God?

CLOSING PRAYER

Heavenly Father, oh, that we would simply believe that what You say is true—both trustworthy and faithful. May Your Spirit in us fully convince us of Your character and empower us to believe and obey. In Jesus' name, we pray, amen.

Day 5 | Reflection

Reflection is a powerful tool for internalizing the things we've learned about God, about how He works, and about ourselves. Begin today by praying and asking God to show you how this week's study specifically applies to your now-and-not-yet life.

Take some time to read through your observations and insights in Days 1–4 of this week's study. What are your top three takeaways from this week? Why?

1.

2.

3.

What truth(s) can you preach to yourself based on this week's study? (List as many things as you can. You may not need to preach all these truths to yourself in your current season, but you never know when they *will* be needed.)

Based on this week's study, complete this sentence:

God is more faithful than I know because _____.

ONE SMALL THING

What is one small, tangible step you can take *in the coming week* to believe what God says is true? It may be as simple as reciting a verse that declares the truth you need to believe or sharing your struggle to believe the truth with a friend. Whatever it is, don't let this week of study pass by without making a practical "resolution" for pressing in. If nothing comes to mind, write a prayer asking God to direct you to take one small step.

CLOSING PRAYER

A Liturgy for When It Feels Impossible
From *Now and Not Yet*

O God, who knows infinitely more than I,
who am I to say what is possible
and what is impossible?
I confess that my metrics measure only
what I think is reasonable, who I believe is worthy, and
how I think my story ought to go.
And when I gauge my qualifications,
I'm tempted to believe
that I'm indispensable or
that my unlikeliness disqualifies me.
Neither is true.
So teach me true humility, O God,
and let me not continue in a distrust of You
that masquerades as modesty.
May I surrender all that makes me seem likely to succeed
and all that renders me unlikely,
offering each to Your service, Lord.
Amen.

God's Sovereignty Directs a Bigger Story

GROUP SESSION

OPENING

Have a volunteer read the opening out loud for the group.

"Sometimes faithfulness to God and his word sets us on a course where circumstances get worse, not better. It is then that knowing God's promises and his ways are crucial."[1]

It feels painful to say out loud, but whether we've experienced it personally or observed it from the outside, we've probably all wondered about what this quote says is true: sometimes, even when we're wholeheartedly following the Lord, things get worse . . . more difficult . . . more painful.

Have you ever walked through a season like that?

When it feels like everything is getting hard, where do we turn? What promises of God do we need to know? How can knowing His ways truly sustain us?

That's what we're exploring today: the faithfulness of God in situations that don't make any sense to us.

SCRIPTURE: GENESIS 37:1–4

Open your Bibles and have a volunteer read this week's Scripture out loud for the group. It doesn't matter which translation you have—reading God's Word together is always a good idea!

WARM-UP QUESTION

Take a few moments to think about the question individually before asking for one or two volunteers to share their answers with the group.

Have you ever walked through a season where following God felt like a series of circumstances that got worse over time? What did it feel like?

WATCH THE SESSION TWO VIDEO

Scripture referenced in this session:
Genesis 37:3–5, 12–36; 39:2–6, 21–23; 41:39; 50:20

Feel free to use this space to take notes.

GROUP DISCUSSION QUESTIONS

Use the following questions to help process the themes from the video session. You may not get to every question and that's okay!

1. What areas of your life are you tempted to believe that God has forgotten about? Is there anything it feels like He's silent about?

2. What part of Joseph's story resonates with you the most? Why?

3. How would you describe the sovereignty of God in your own life? Where do you see it? Where are you tempted to doubt it?

4. What life, family, job, house, gifts, talents, or resources can you steward *today*?

5. Who or what comes to mind when you think about "faithful stewardship"?

PRAY

Spend some time praying together before dismissing the group.

> *Jesus, thank You for the story of Joseph—for how we see Your sovereignty so clearly and for his example of faithful stewardship. Help us to both see and savor Your sovereignty in our own lives this week. May we use each instance as a deposit to withdraw from in seasons that tempt us to doubt redemption is possible. Amen.*

HOMEWORK

Set aside time this week to work through the personal study on the following pages. The personal study will unpack themes from today's teaching and help you delve deeper into God's Word. Do as much as you can to get the full benefit!

God's Sovereignty Directs a Bigger Story

PERSONAL STUDY

SESSION TWO OBJECTIVES:

- Explore what God's Word says about His sovereignty.
- See the life of Joseph through the lens of God's sovereignty.
- Discover God's faithfulness on display in how He accomplishes His purposes.
- Respond to God's faithfulness by reflecting on ways we can steward what's in front of us.

This week's study draws on themes from chapter 4 of *Now and Not Yet*.

Day 1 | God Is Sovereign

Before you begin today's study, take a moment to quiet your mind and pray. Ask God to teach you from His Word, and ask the Holy Spirit to help you apply that truth to your life.

Wrapping our brains around limitless control or the ability to make our plans actually happen is tough because, as much as we wish we did, we have no personal experience with this type of power or authority. (In all honestly, because I know myself, I know that *not* having total power or authority is definitely a good thing!) But there *is* One who is the very definition of power and authority to control *all* things: God. This limitless control and authority to act is known as His sovereignty.

> *God's sovereignty means that His rule over all creation is absolute. Nothing can overrule Him or happen outside of His plans.*[1]

Today, we're going to explore some passages that point to and describe His sovereignty. But first, I want you to write down some thoughts.

When you hear the phrase "the sovereignty of God," what comes to mind?

How would you characterize your emotional response to the sovereignty of God? (circle one)

MOSTLY NEGATIVE   MOSTLY NEUTRAL   MOSTLY POSITIVE   UNDECIDED

What do you think is the biggest contributing factor to your emotional response?

My prayer is that today's study helps paint a glorious picture of what it means for God to be sovereign and that we see it as the gift it truly is. So, let's get started.

DIGGING DEEPER

As I've already alluded to, one way to think about the sovereignty of God is to think about it as a combination of His absolute authority and His absolute control.

God holds authority *because he is our* author. *As Creator, God has ultimate authority over all of creation and he only uses it for good.*[2]

God's control *is limitless—He doesn't just control some* things, *He controls* all *things.*

In other words, nothing is outside of His control, *and* He is the ultimate source of authority.

There are lots of aspects of God's sovereignty that we don't have enough time to delve into today . . . questions like, "If God ultimately controls everything, does what we do matter?" and, "How does God's authority and control account for evil?"

These are great questions that I encourage you to dig into or discuss with a pastor or trusted mentor in your life! But, for the sake of our study today, we're primarily going to look for answers to these three questions:

- Who or what is God sovereign over?
- What adjectives would you use to describe the nature of God's sovereignty?
- What is an appropriate response to God's sovereignty?

Read the following passages and circle which component of His sovereignty is being described (hint: it may be both!). Write out any observations you make about God's sovereignty in the passage, and then we'll return to the three questions I just posed.

READ	CIRCLE COMPONENT(S)	OBSERVATIONS ABOUT GOD'S SOVEREIGNTY
Psalm 115:3	Authority Control	
Lamentations 3:37–39	Authority Control	
Ephesians 1:3–12	Authority Control	
Romans 8:26–28	Authority Control	
Isaiah 46:8–10	Authority Control	
Psalm 103:19	Authority Control	
Colossians 1:16–18	Authority Control	
Psalm 139	Authority Control	
Job 42:1–2	Authority Control	
Proverbs 19:21	Authority Control	

Look at your observations. What stands out to you?

Now, answer these three questions:

Who or what is God sovereign over?

What adjectives would you use to describe the nature of God's sovereignty?

What is an appropriate response to God's sovereignty?

Friend, God's sovereignty is such a *big* concept! But such an important one for understanding who He is and how He interacts with us. The foundation of understanding you've built today will serve us well as we look at the life of Joseph tomorrow and ultimately see God's faithfulness.

GETTING PERSONAL

Look back at your answer to the first question you answered today. Has your understanding of God's sovereignty changed after today's study? If so, how?

Which aspect of God's sovereignty is most challenging for you to personally submit to? (circle one)

GOD'S AUTHORITY   GOD'S CONTROL

Why?

What areas of life are you most likely to fight for control in? What does it look like in your daily life? (Example: I want to control how others view me. I sometimes spend too much on clothes I think other people will approve of.)

Is your heart currently positioned to respond appropriately to the sovereignty of God? If not, what would it take to shift it?

CLOSING PRAYER

Lord, Your sovereignty is sometimes hard for my finite mind to comprehend, but I am so grateful for what I do understand. Help me submit to Your authority and control, especially when it comes to _____.
In Jesus' name, amen.

Day 2 | Joseph's Story: Favor in Hard Places

Before you begin today's study, take a moment to quiet your mind and pray. Ask God to teach you from His Word and ask the Holy Spirit to help you apply that truth to your life.

STUDY TIP

Remember, the second day of each week's study is designed to help you see a big-picture story of one person's life. To get the big picture, we'll primarily be reading (a lot!) of Scripture and making observations. This context is what we'll draw on for the rest of the week, so take your time and feel free to split up today's study over more than one day if that serves you well.

Much like we did with Abraham, today we're reading texts that tell us about the life of Joseph. His story spans several chapters of the Bible (much of Genesis 37–50!) and is full of twists and turns. It's a story that gets worse before it gets better, but as we'll see over the next couple of days, it's a story that shows us the faithful sovereignty of God in incredible ways.

1. The Beloved Son

Read Genesis 37:1–11. Summarize Joseph's relationship with his father.

Summarize Joseph's relationship with his brothers.

2. Sold into Slavery

Read Genesis 37:12–36. What did the brothers initially plan for Joseph?

Who intervened?

What was the result for Joseph?

3. Steadfast Integrity

Read Genesis 39:1–23. Where does Joseph end up?

How did the Lord provide for Joseph in Potiphar's house (verses 2–4)?

Summarize what happened with Potiphar's wife.

How did the Lord provide for Joseph in prison (verse 21)?

3. Dream Interpreter

Read Genesis 40:1–23. Who does Joseph interpret dreams for?

What did Joseph ask the cupbearer for in verse 14?

Do Joseph's interpretations come true?

Does the cupbearer honor Joseph's request?

4. Second-in-Command

Read Genesis 41:1–41. (Hang in there, friend! I know this is a lot of reading, but I'm praying that you engage fully with this epic story!)

How much time does this chapter say has passed since Joseph interpreted the dreams of his fellow prisoners (verse 1)?

When Joseph is summoned by Pharoah, how does he answer Pharoah's question about whether Joseph can interpret his dream (verse 16)?

Summarize the meaning of Pharoah's dreams as interpreted by Joseph.

How does Pharoah describe Joseph in verse 38?

What position does Pharoah give Joseph as a result?

5. God Provides

Read Genesis 41:46–56. How does Joseph steward Egypt's crops?

6. Reunited

Read Genesis 45:4–15. Who does Joseph credit with his current circumstance?

For what purpose?

When Potiphar hears that Joseph's family has come, he suggests that Joseph bring his entire family to live in Egypt so that he can continue to provide for them through the famine. So that's what they do.

Israel's whole household relocates to Egypt (where they'll remain for the next four hundred years, as we'll see next week).

When Israel eventually dies, Joseph's brothers worry that he will finally exact revenge on them for the way they sold him into slavery as a teen.

Read Joseph's response to their concerns in Genesis 50:19–21. Summarize his response.

How would you summarize Joseph's "not yet"?

GETTING PERSONAL

What part(s) of Joseph's story, if any, resonates with your own experience?

What habits, practices, or rhythms might help you cultivate a heart bent toward responding as Joseph did to his brothers?

CLOSING PRAYER

Lord, though Joseph's story contains so many difficult pieces—betrayal, injustice, being forgotten—Your hand is all over his story. Your presence and favor are continually with him and clearly seen by the people around him. Thank You for always being with us . . . even when it feels like things may be moving from bad to worse, help us remember that You are in control. That whatever You will, You will do, and that nothing can thwart Your plans. Help us see Your sovereignty in our own lives, even as we observe it in Joseph's! In Jesus' name, amen.

Day 3 | God's Faithfulness on Display: A Bigger Story

I can't help but read Joseph's story and wonder what was going through his mind on any given day of his life. Surely, he wondered what good could possibly come from his brothers' hatred, his slavery in Egypt, and his years spent in prison for a crime he didn't commit. And even after his rise to power, second only to Pharoah, I wonder if he ever asked, "Why, Lord?"

One of the most amazing things about Joseph's story is actually how integral it is to a bigger story that a sovereign God is writing.

Return with me to the covenant God made with Abraham in Genesis 15.

Read Genesis 15:12–14. What does God tell Abraham about his offspring?

How long does He say they will be afflicted?

Now, read Genesis 46:1–7. Note that Jacob (Israel) is leaving the land that God had promised Abraham and his offspring! What does God tell Jacob He will do in Egypt?

God used Joseph as a means to bring His chosen people to a new place: Egypt. In Egypt, they grew to be a strong *nation*—so strong, in fact, that a future Pharoah would fear their power and enslave them. God's people cried out, and He heard them and sent Moses to lead them out of Egypt. (We'll look into this part of the story next week!)

Read Exodus 12:40–41. How long did the Israelites live in Egypt?

Is your mind blown yet?! Joseph's story is part of God's *much bigger story*. He is **one piece** of God's sovereign plan. An integral piece to the story of God's people.

Follow the plotline with me:

- Joseph's brothers hated him and sold him into slavery.

- He ends up in the house of the captain of Pharoah's guard.

- He is imprisoned with Pharoah's cupbearer, whose dream he interprets.

- The cupbearer eventually remembers Joseph's gift.

- God gives Joseph the ability to interpret Pharoah's dream, as well as the ability to make and execute a plan to survive a famine.

- Joseph becomes second-in-command only to Pharoah.

- The famine brings Joseph's family to Egypt.

- Joseph's family (the family of Israel, his father) is rescued from starvation by moving from Canaan (the land promised) to Egypt.

And God told Abraham about it in the very beginning.

God's absolute authority and absolute control are all over Joseph's story . . . even though he had no idea. He couldn't have imagined how he fit into God's sovereign plan on any given day of his life. But he did. And God was purposeful.

Friend, can I remind you? God's sovereignty is *always* purposeful.

MORE FAITHFUL THAN YOU KNOW: A TYPE OF JESUS

We can't leave the story of Joseph without uncovering another layer of God's sovereign purpose.

Let's start by defining what may be new terms for you:

- A *type* is a symbol of something future and distant, something that is yet to come. Types point us toward antitypes.

- An *antiype* is the thing that is coming.

As we read the Old Testament, specifically, we can observe several *types* of Jesus—people or things that point us to Him before He is physically present on earth. In some way, these characters or things foreshadow Jesus, by character, word, or deed.

BIBLE FACT
Other Old Testament types include Adam, Abraham, Moses, Samuel, and David, among others. And as it turns out, Joseph is a *type* of Jesus.

Read the verses and passages listed below and write down the ways Joseph is a *type* who points us to Jesus, the *antitype*. The first two are filled in for you as examples.

JOSEPH	JESUS	HOW IS JOSEPH A *TYPE* OF JESUS?
Genesis 37:2	John 10:14	Both are shepherds.
Genesis 37:3	Matthew 3:17	Both are beloved sons of their father.
Genesis 37:4–5	John 1:11, 7:5	
Genesis 37:36	Philippians 2:6–7	
Genesis 39:19–20	John 18:38–39	
Genesis 41:39–40	Philippians 2:9–11	
Genesis 41:54, 57	John 3:16	

Friend, I hope this quick study of Joseph as a *type* of Jesus leads you to worship!

Do you see it? Joseph is not only part of God's sovereign plan for the nation of Israel, but he also points us to Jesus Himself! God's sovereignty is limitless, and His control is unmatched!

> *"I have a point of view. You have a point of view. God has view."*[1]

GETTING PERSONAL

What emotions does today's study bring up for you? Why?

In what ways might this change the way you navigate your not-yet-wonderful circumstances?

How might today's study change the way you pray about your not-yet-wonderful circumstances?

CLOSING PRAYER

Lord Jesus, we are in awe of Your sovereignty and of the way Your plans unfold. Forgive us for the ways we let our limited view of the story of our lives dictate our level of trust toward You. Help us to consider, even when we can't imagine there is purpose in our present circumstances, that You are writing a much bigger story. Empower us, by Your Spirit, to rest in Your sovereignty. In your name, we pray, amen.

Day 4 | Steward What's in Front of You

Now that we've explored the depths of God's sovereignty, read the story of Joseph's life, and seen God's faithfulness on display in the ways His sovereignty accomplishes His purposes, let's take a step back to consider how Joseph can be an example for us today.

What is it that we can take away from the way Joseph walked with God amid his not-yet-wonderful circumstances?

JOSEPH'S EXAMPLE

Using your notes and observations from day 2, remind yourself how Joseph responded to or walked with God throughout his life. What was his primary role, task, or action in each season of his life?

SEASON	JOSEPH'S PRIMARY ROLE, TASK, OR ACTION
The Beloved Son	
Sold into Slavery	
Steadfast Integrity	
Dream Interpreter	
Second-in-Command	
Reunited	

How would you summarize or characterize Joseph's posture toward God based on what we've read this week?

There are likely lots of words and phrases that come to mind—humble, long-suffering, honest, servant-hearted—but there's one word that really stands out to me: **steward.**

Regardless of where he was, what circumstances he was navigating, or what promises had been broken, Joseph *stewards* every task or opportunity put before him . . . even while he waits for God's plan to unfold. He rested in God's sovereignty by doing the work in front of him, *stewarding* every opportunity.

DEFINITION

According to Vine's Expository Dictionary, a *steward* is defined as "the manager of a household or estate."[1] Joseph is often referenced as a classic biblical example of a steward because of the work he did in Potiphar's house.

I don't know about you, but when every aspect of life seems to be trending for the worse, my first instinct isn't always to faithfully tend to the tasks in front of me. But that's exactly what Joseph did.

As a slave, he stewarded the affairs of Potiphar's house.

As a prisoner, he stewarded the tasks assigned to him by the prison guard.

As a dream interpreter, he stewarded the interpretation God gave him for Pharoah.

As a second-in-command of Egypt, he stewarded the resources of a nation.

And he did it *diligently.*

Whether you think of yourself as a "steward" or not, the reality is that we're all stewards with responsibilities to a Master, much like Joseph was to Potiphar.

THE MASTER

Read each of the following passages and write down your observations about who the Master is and what He owns or possesses.

READ	OBSERVATIONS
Deuteronomy 10:14	
Psalm 24:1–2	
Romans 11:36	
1 Corinthians 4:7	

Summarize your observations.

THE STEWARD

Now, let's look at a parable that gives us insight into the role and responsibilities of stewards.

Read Matthew 25:14–30. What did the master give his servants?

What did he ask them to oversee, or steward (verse 14)?

BIBLE FACT

A talent was a monetary unit worth about twenty years' wages for a common laborer.[2]

Fill out the table.

	WHAT DID THE SERVANT DO WITH HIS TALENTS?	HOW DID THE MASTER RESPOND?
Servant with five talents		
Servant with two talents		
Servant with one talent		

Which servant(s) was a faithful steward of his master's wealth?

Notice that the master wasn't as concerned about how much money each servant made as he was with how the servant *stewarded* the opportunity.

Think about how this applies to you and me. If God truly is sovereign, holding absolute power and authority over *all* things, then you and I are simply stewards of His wealth! This means that *everything* we've been given—our gifts, resources, time, personality, families, friends, jobs, and opportunities—can be stewarded for His glory.

The question that remains is: Will you steward what you've been given?

Oh, that our stewardship would result in hearing, "Well done, good and faithful servant" from our Master!

GETTING PERSONAL

What gifts has God given you? Think about how you're wired, what you're good at, what you enjoy, and what you have to offer when it comes to serving others.

What circumstances has God put before you in this season of life?

What are the natural tasks for those circumstances?

How would you rate yourself on a scale of 1 (not stewarding my gifts at all) to 5 (stewarding my gifts consistently and effectively) when it comes to your current stewardship?

| 1 | 2 | 3 | 4 | 5 |

What would help you steward your gifts most effectively?

CLOSING PRAYER

Use the following sentence starters as a springboard to write your own personal prayer today:

Lord, You are the Creator and owner of everything! Help me remember that You are the master and I am Your steward.

I confess that when it comes to stewarding my gifts, I . . .

Thank you for Joseph's example of diligent stewardship. Help me to . . .

In Jesus' name, I pray, amen.

Day 5 | Reflection

Reflection is a powerful tool for internalizing the things we've learned about God, about how He works, and about ourselves. Begin today by praying and asking God to show you how this week's study specifically applies to your now-and-not-yet life.

Another week down, and another opportunity to reflect on all that God, by His Spirit, has shown you this week!

Take some time to read through your observations and insights in Days 1–4 of this week's study. What are your top three takeaways from this week?

What truth(s) can you preach to yourself based on this week's study? (List as many things as you can. You may not need to preach all these truths to yourself in your current season, but you never know when they *will* be needed.)

Based on this week's study, complete this sentence:

God is more faithful than I know because _____.

ONE SMALL THING

What is one small, tangible step you can take *in the coming week* to steward what's in front of you? It may be as simple as taking inventory of what gifts God has given you or taking inventory of what opportunities are in front of you. Whatever it is, don't let this week of study pass by without making a practical "resolution" for pressing in. If nothing comes to mind, write a prayer asking God to direct you to take one small step.

CLOSING PRAYER

A Liturgy for When You're Waiting on Growth
From *Now and Not Yet*

I am not a Master Gardener.
I don't cause the rain to fall,
or the sun to shine,
or the seeds to germinate.
Forgive me, O Lord, when I mistake the plow in my hand
for a scepter that belongs only to You.
Help me not to dismiss small beginnings.
Teach me to be faithful in the seemingly fruitless tasks,
the everyday mundane, and the hard soil of my life.
When I'm eager to shortcut my way to fruitfulness,
remind me how sweet it is to remain on the vine,
abiding in You.
Apart from You, I can do nothing.
Let me not miss the tasks before me today.
Help me let go of my own ideas of what it means to be fruitful
and instead look to You for the fruit only You can produce.
The sink-full
of dirty dishes, the load of laundry,
the meals to make, the hearts that need tending.
You can and will use every simple act of faithfulness
to sow fruitfulness into my life.
Help me steward what I've been given this day
that You might grow me into Your likeness,
that what flourishes from this season
will make much of Your faithfulness
and less of my fruitfulness.
Amen.

God Provides in the Wilderness

GROUP SESSION

OPENING

Have a volunteer read the opening out loud for the group.

Have you ever walked in the desert for any length of time?

Hot, dry air.

Dusty sand everywhere.

Little to no shelter from the blazing sun.

It might feel like an adventure for a little while, but rest assured it gets old quickly. And, without proper supplies and preparation, the desert can be deadly.

So, isn't it interesting that this is the place God leads His people to? The place He guides them around for forty years? Today, we're entering into the nation of Israel's desert story . . . because the faithfulness of God is always on display, even in the desert.

SCRIPTURE: EXODUS 16:2–5

Open your Bibles and have a volunteer read this week's Scripture out loud for the group. It doesn't matter which translation you have—reading God's Word together is always a good idea!

WARM-UP QUESTION

Take a few moments to think about the question individually before asking for one or two volunteers to share their answers with the group.

What's one way you've seen God tangibly provide, either for yourself or for someone you know? How did it affect your willingness to trust Him later on?

WATCH THE SESSION THREE VIDEO

Scripture referenced in this session: Exodus 1:8–11; 2:23–25; 3:7–9; 13:21–22; 14:21–22; 16:3; Numbers 13:27–28; 14:11; Deuteronomy 8:2–4, 11–18; Matthew 6:25–32

Feel free to use this space to take notes.

GROUP DISCUSSION QUESTIONS

Use the following questions to help process the themes from the video session. You may not get to every question, and that's okay!

1. Have you ever walked through a "desert season"? What was difficult about it?

2. How have you experienced God's presence in desert seasons?

3. Is your natural inclination to remember and trust God's provision, or forget and complain?

4. What habits, rhythms, or practices help you remember how God has provided?

5. What do you need to choose to remember and rehearse about God's faithfulness in the past?

PRAY

Spend some time praying together before dismissing the group.

Father, we are far more like the nation of Israel than we care to admit, panicking instead of remembering Your provision and complaining while we wait in the desert. Thank You that You are our Provider—that You have promised to meet our needs just like You met Israel's needs. Help us trust You, every day. In Jesus' name, we pray, amen.

HOMEWORK

Set aside time this week to work through the personal study on the following pages. The personal study will unpack themes from today's teaching and help you delve deeper into God's Word. Do as much as you can to get the full benefit!

God Provides in the Wilderness

PERSONAL STUDY

SESSION THREE OBJECTIVES:

- Discover what God's Word tells us about how He's a Provider.
- Explore Israel's exodus from Egypt and time in the wilderness.
- See God's faithfulness on display in the daily manna He provided for Israel.
- Respond to God's faithfulness by remembering how He's provided in the past.

> This week's study draws on themes from chapters 1 and 8 of *Now and Not Yet*.

Day 1 | God Provides

Before you begin today's study, take a moment to quiet your mind and pray. Ask God to teach you from His Word, and ask the Holy Spirit to help you apply that truth to your life.

Do you remember the first time you truly had to "provide for" yourself? Maybe when you went to college, or when you moved into your first apartment or started your first "adult" job? Remember what it felt like when you realized that it was up to you to grocery shop, meal prep, and clean up? And when there were actual bills to pay on a regular basis?

Even if you'd longed for independence, I'm guessing it required some time for you to settle into the role. If you're anything like me, you probably made some mistakes along the way, too—forgetting to pay a bill on time, or running out of a kitchen staple in the middle of the week. We all had to learn how to provide for ourselves.

But that's not how it is with God. He is the very definition of provider! And not just any provider—a perfect provider. He knows every need and is perfectly able to meet every need.

*God's provision shows that He is intimately involved
in the lives of His people and is their Sustainer.*[1]

We'll see how God's provision plays out in the story of the nation of Israel's exodus from Egypt (spoiler alert: it's amazing!), but first let's explore what we see about God as Provider throughout all of Scripture.

DIGGING DEEPER

Often, you can learn a lot about a word or phrase by studying the first time it is used in the Bible. This study method is called the First Mention Principle and we're going to employ it today!

The very first time God is referred to as Provider is in a story we referenced in week one—with our old friend, Abraham.

Read Genesis 22:1–14. Verse 14 tells us that Abraham calls the place "Jehovah Jireh," which translates to "The Lord Will Provide." What is it that God provided?

On the surface, God provided a ram, right? Pause for a moment to consider what *else* God provided for through the ram:

- A substitute for Isaac's death
- A sacrifice to atone for sin
- A covenant promise

Based on this short list and any other insights the Lord may impress on you, what observations can you make about the nature of God's provision for Abraham?

Using the First Mention Principle, what inferences can you make about the nature of God's provision in general?

Now, let's explore a few other passages that feature God as a provider. As you read each one, make note of what He's providing and to whom He is providing it.

READ	WHAT DOES GOD PROVIDE?	FOR WHOM?
Psalm 104:27–30		
Matthew 6:25–33		
Matthew 7:7–11		
2 Corinthians 9:6–11		
Psalm 34:8–10		
2 Peter 1:3–4		
Matthew 11:28–30		
John 3:16–17		
Proverbs 3:5–6		
James 1:5–6		

In a few sentences, summarize the nature of God's provision for His people. (It might be helpful to think about how you'd describe to a child how God provides.)

YOUR GREATEST NEED

Our everyday needs—wisdom for relationships, marriage, or parenting, a job that helps us pay our bills, physical shelter, sustenance, etc.—are the needs that tend to take up most of our attention. But, friend, can I remind you that your biggest need has *already* been met by our Provider God?

Read Romans 3:23. What is the biggest problem every human faces?

Read Romans 6:23. What does our common plight destine us for?

Read Romans 5:6–8. How does Jesus meet our needs?

Read Romans 5:1–2 and Romans 8:1. What's the result of accepting Jesus' death as payment for our sin?

A NOTE

Friend, I hope these verses are familiar to you, and that walking through them brings you much joy! However, if these verses are new to you, and you're unsure if your greatest need truly has been met by Christ, I encourage you to flip to the back of this study and read Appendix A for further explanation.

Our sin is cause for eternal separation from God, but in His sovereign plan, Jesus steps in to pay the price for sin and gives us the ability to be reconciled to God forever. Praise the Lord!

Now, with all these passages in Romans tucked into your heart, write out Romans 8:32:

How will God also give us *all* things? Our God provides!

GETTING PERSONAL

How have you seen God provide, either in your own life or in someone else's?

Is there any specific thing you find hard to believe that God will provide? Why?

What is the number one thing you're asking God to provide in your current season?

What's one verse from today's study that you should consider memorizing?

Use the following prompts as a springboard for your own personal prayer to close your time today.

Father, thank You for all the ways You provide for me. I am so grateful for . . .

Help me trust Your provision in my not-yet situation, as I wait for . . .

Thank You for Your Word that tells me who You are! In Jesus' name, amen.

Day 2 | Israel's Story: Doubt in the Desert

Before you begin today's study, take a moment to quiet your mind and pray. Ask God to teach you from His Word, and ask the Holy Spirit to help you apply that truth to your life.

STUDY TIP
Remember, the second day of each week's study is designed to help you see a big-picture story of one person's life. In order to get the big picture, we'll primarily be reading (a lot!) of Scripture and making observations. This context is what we'll draw on for the rest of the week, so take your time and feel free to split up today's study over more than one day if that serves you well.

Today, we're exploring the story of Israel, beginning with their exodus from Egypt all the way through the forty years they spent in the desert.

1. Slaves in Egypt

Read Exodus 1:1–14 and 2:23. Summarize the Israelites' position in Egypt.

What did they do as a result?

How did God respond?

Why did God respond?

2. Protected from Plagues

Read Exodus 7:14–25. Summarize the first plague.

How do verses 14 and 22 describe Pharoah's heart?

Read Exodus 12:1–32. Summarize what God asked Israel to do to save their firstborns from the last plague.

What did God promise to do if they obeyed (verse 23)?

What is Pharoah's response to the last plague?

3. The Exodus

Read Exodus 12:33–42. Describe how the Israelites left Egypt.

How many people were there?

BIBLE FACT

Though there's some debate, some scholars believe that the number of men (600,000), in addition to the number of women and children, means that upwards of one million people left Egypt after the first Passover.

How long had they been in Egypt? (Remember the significance of this number from week 2?)

Read Exodus 13:17–22. What does God provide for Israel as a tangible sign of His presence right away?

Read Exodus 14:5–31. Summarize what happened at the Red Sea.

4. Daily Provision

Read Exodus 15:24–26. What does God provide?

What does God promise the people?

Read Exodus 16:2–8. What does God say He will provide in the morning?

What does God say He will provide in the evening?

5. Hesitation + Disobedience

Read Numbers 13:1–2, 21–33. Summarize what the spies report.

What is their specific concern?

Read Numbers 14:1–4. Summarize the Israelites' response to the report.

Read Numbers 14:26–30. What is God's response to the people's unwillingness to take the land He has already promised them?

6. The Desert

Read Numbers 11:4–15. What are the people complaining about?

Read Numbers 20:2–9. What are the people complaining about?

A NOTE

Wilderness seasons in our lives are *not* always a direct result of disobedience or a lack of faith. Those attitudes happen to be why God brought the Israelites to the desert, but that's not the only reason He might have for bringing you to a wilderness season.

Read Deuteronomy 8:2–4, 8–11. What does Moses instruct the people to remember?

Though we've covered *a lot* of territory here (you did it, friend!), we're definitely not covering all of Israel's story this week—this is, in fact, only the beginning. God's chosen people have a long and winding path ahead of them and their story will continue to unfold all the way through the rest of the Bible.

The question I want to focus on at the end of today's (or the last couple of days) study is this: How would you describe Israel's "not-yet" circumstance?

The desert may hold all kinds of danger, but it also teaches God's people a lot about who He is. I can't wait to keep uncovering the ways He provides.

Do you feel like you're currently in a desert season? If so, how? If not, have you ever navigated a desert season? What was it like?

What are you most likely to complain about in your current season (regardless of whether it's a desert season)?

What past provision from God do you need to remember today?

CLOSING PRAYER

Father, thank You for teaching us about who You are and about who we are through the story of Israel. Help us to be people who remember Your provision instead of complaining about what we think we lack. You are a good Father who always provides what His children need . . . help us to trust You instead of doubting You. In Jesus' name, we pray, amen.

Day 3 | God's Faithfulness
on Display: Manna

Today we're going to focus on one particular expression of God's provision for Israel while they were in the desert: manna.

First, let's see what God's Word says about manna. Read each of the following passages and write down your observations.

READ	OBSERVATIONS ABOUT MANNA
Exodus 16:4–5	
Exodus 16:13–21	
Exodus 16:31	
Exodus 16:35	
Numbers 11:7–9	

Summarize what manna is.

Now, let's see about how manna is to be remembered by Israel.

Read Deuteronomy 8:3, 16. Besides physical sustenance, what purpose did manna serve for Israel?

Read Joshua 5:12. When did God stop providing manna?

Here are a few observations I want to highlight for you.

1. **Manna was a specific provision for a specific situation.** As we just read, manna was entirely new to the nation of Israel. It wasn't a food they were familiar with or had ever eaten before. They had absolutely nothing to do with its production—they simply had to gather it. God knew what they needed, how much they needed, and His provision even accounted for their Sabbath rest!

2. **Manna met an urgent physical need.** Though we know the people grew tired of it and complained about it, I love the simplicity of God's plan for people's physical needs. As we saw in Deuteronomy, God was ultimately after the people's hearts in the desert . . . but that didn't mean He overlooked their everyday, tangible needs.

3. **Manna came daily.** When you think about how many people needed food on a daily basis for forty years . . . the amount of manna God provided is staggering! Every day, for forty years, whether they collected it that day or not, **God provided**. They couldn't gather more than they needed for the day or it would spoil, unless they were accounting for Sabbath, when it would *not* spoil overnight. It's miraculous!

MORE FAITHFUL THAN YOU KNOW: HOW MANNA POINTS US TO JESUS

Much like the story of Joseph showed us a *type* of Jesus last week, manna is a symbol that points us directly to Christ.

Read John 6:47–51. Summarize the comparison Jesus makes between manna and Himself.

Here's a chart that makes a few additional comparisons for you. If you have time, I encourage you to read each of the passages and use them as a springboard to praise God.

MANNA	JESUS
. . . was strange and mysterious at first	. . . is the wonder of men and angels both 1 Timothy 3:16
. . . came down from heaven	. . . came down from heaven John 6:35–38
. . . given to all as a free gift	. . . offered salvation to all as a free gift John 3:16, Ephesians 2:8–9

Spend some time reflecting on other comparisons and write down any that come to mind.

Friend, remember that Jesus is the true bread of life! And, more faithful than we know.

GETTING PERSONAL

What "manna" do you long for most in desert seasons?

What manna is God providing for you right now?

CLOSING PRAYER

Father God, You are so kind! You faithfully provided manna for every day Israel spent in the desert. They were hungry and out of options, and You took care of them. Thank You for the story of their dependence and Your provision and for all the ways it points us to Jesus—Your greatest provision for us in the desert of our sin. Give us eyes to see today's "manna" in the places we're waiting on You for something that has yet to resolve. We love You, God! In Jesus' name, we pray, amen.

Day 4 | Remember His Provision

As we've already alluded to this week, we like to distance ourselves from Israel's responses to God—trying to convince ourselves that we would have responded differently. But the truth is, we're not all that different. We forget all the ways God has provided, just like Israel did.

So, what's the remedy? Read each of the following passages and observe the instructions given:

READ	OBSERVATIONS
Deuteronomy 5:15	
Deuteronomy 6:12	
Deuteronomy 7:18	
Deuteronomy 8:2, 18	
Isaiah 46:9	
Psalm 77:11	
Psalm 143:5	
Psalm 103:2	
1 Chronicles 16:8–13	

Do you see a theme emerging? With this many reminders, it's clear that forgetting is our default and remembering takes an intentional effort.

Consciously recalling—*remembering*—how we have already seen God at work in our lives is one of the best ways to cultivate continued trust in His ability to provide in the future.

"Count your blessings, name them one by one, count your many blessings, see what God has done."[1]

GETTING PERSONAL

So, let's practice remembering together! In the rest of your time today, I want you to spend some time reflecting on and recording ways you have experienced God's provision in your life. It may be for something you needed, or for something you just wanted or desired. It can be a spiritual need God met for you, or something more tangible and physical. It may be that He provided wisdom, clarity, a friend, a place, comfort, finances, a job . . . anything! Recall His faithfulness to you in the way He has provided for you.

EXAMPLE: REMEMBERING GOD'S PROVISION

NEED OR DESIRE	A way to be reconciled to God
HOW GOD PROVIDED	Sent Jesus to die on the cross and pay the penalty for my sin
WHAT YOU LEARNED ABOUT GOD	He loves me and wants to be in a relationship with me
HOW GOD USED THE SITUATION IN YOUR LIFE	To give me eternal life, to equip me with the Holy Spirit as I live a life of faith

A NOTE

The example I provided is applicable for anyone who has put their trust in Jesus' death and resurrection for salvation. If you've not made a decision to follow Jesus but want to learn more about what that means, please read Appendix A at the end of this study to hear Jesus' invitation to you!

Your Turn

Before you begin writing, spend a few moments in prayer asking God to remind you of ways He has provided for you in the past. You may or may not need all of the boxes provided, but aim to fill out a chart for at least three examples from your own life. Your need or desire may reflect a spiritual, emotional, or physical need—nothing is off-limits as you recall God's provision in your own life!

REMEMBERING GOD'S PROVISION

NEED OR DESIRE	
HOW GOD PROVIDED	
WHAT YOU LEARNED ABOUT GOD	
HOW GOD USED THE SITUATION IN YOUR LIFE	

NEED OR DESIRE	
HOW GOD PROVIDED	
WHAT YOU LEARNED ABOUT GOD	
HOW GOD USED THE SITUATION IN YOUR LIFE	

NEED OR DESIRE	
HOW GOD PROVIDED	
WHAT YOU LEARNED ABOUT GOD	
HOW GOD USED THE SITUATION IN YOUR LIFE	

As you wrap up this exercise, return to the Lord in prayer. Write a prayer specifically thanking Him for all the provisions you just wrote down. Acknowledge that your list barely scratches the surface, and ask Him for help to *remember* what He's done.

CLOSING PRAYER

Lord, the depth and breadth and width of Your provision in our lives is truly astounding! Thank You for helping us recall the ways You've met us in both big and small ways. Help us to be people who consistently and intentionally remember Your faithfulness! May it cultivate, build, and strengthen our trust in You for every not-yet-wonderful circumstance we face. In Jesus' name, we pray, amen.

Day 5 | Reflection

Reflection is a powerful tool for internalizing the things we've learned about God, about how He works, and about ourselves. Begin today by praying and asking God to show you how this week's study specifically applies to your now-and-not-yet life.

We're halfway through the study, and I'm so grateful for your diligence in studying God's Word!

Take some time to read through your observations and insights in Days 1–4 of this week's study. What are your top three takeaways from this week?

What truth(s) can you preach to yourself based on this week's study? (List as many things as you can. You may not need to preach all these truths to yourself in your current season, but you never know when they *will* be needed.)

Based on this week's study, complete this sentence:

God is more faithful than I know because _____.

ONE SMALL THING

What is one small, tangible step you can take *in the coming week* to remember His provision? It may be as simple as writing a list of ways you've seen God provide or singing a worship song to give thanks. Whatever it is, don't let this week of study pass by without making a practical "resolution" for pressing in. If nothing comes to mind, write a prayer asking God to direct you to take one small step.

CLOSING PRAYER

A Liturgy for When There's No End in Sight
From *Now and Not Yet*

O Lord, You made us to thirst for You alone,
and yet, in the desert places of our lives,
we're prone to believe that something less than
Living Water will do.
No wonder You chose to take Your people through,
instead of around, the desert.
How else would we discover that You are enough
when we experience
desolation,
desperation,
and desertion?
May I not wander aimlessly in my desert, O Lord.
Give me sustenance from the manna of Your Word.
Let me rehearse it, savor it, and return to it
like one who does not forget a satisfying meal.
Use the harshness of my current location, vocation,
or relationships to extricate me from
the false gods of comfort, ease, and abundance.
Woo my heart to greater dependency on
the oasis of Your care for me.
Amen.

God Hears Your Cries

GROUP SESSION

OPENING

Have a volunteer read the opening out loud for the group.

Sometimes the best way to show our friends, family, children, roommates, or coworkers that we care about them is to just *listen* to what they have to say. That unhurried type of listening, where you're actually hearing the words coming from their mouths instead of letting your mind wander or focusing on what you want to tell them next.

There's something really powerful about being loved by being seen and heard. And, on the flip side, there's something really painful about feeling unseen and misunderstood.

Today, we're beginning our exploration of the life of Hannah, who at various points in her story likely felt emotions on both ends of this spectrum. The beauty in Hannah's example is that regardless of how she felt, she continued to talk to and trust the Lord. She allowed her not-yet-wonderful circumstance to lead her straight to her all-knowing God, instead of away from Him.

And ultimately, God saw her, heard her, and remembered her. Let's see what we can learn from her example!

SCRIPTURE: 1 SAMUEL 1:12–18

Open your Bibles and have a volunteer read this week's Scripture out loud for the group. It doesn't matter which translation you have—reading God's Word together is always a good idea!

WARM-UP QUESTION

Take a few moments to think about the question individually before asking for one or two volunteers to share their answers with the group.

Think about a time you clearly felt *heard* or *seen* by the Lord. What happened? How did it make you feel?

WATCH THE SESSION FOUR VIDEO

Scripture referenced in this session: 1 Samuel 1:1-19; 1 Peter 5:5-7; Psalm 139:1-4; 34:15-18; James 4:10; Proverbs 3:5-6

Feel free to use this space to take notes.

GROUP DISCUSSION QUESTIONS

Use the following questions to help process the themes from the video session. You may not get to every question and that's okay!

1. Have you ever felt like Hannah? In what way(s)?

2. Have you ever prayed for the same request over a long period of time? If so, what was your experience like?

3. Do you believe that God truly knows *all* things? Do your actions align with your stated belief? If not, what would greater alignment require from you?

4. How would you describe your current posture before the Lord? Would you say it leans more toward surrender or more toward clenched fists when it comes to your not-yet circumstance?

5. What do you think surrendering your pain or desire for control would entail? What's your biggest obstacle to surrender?

PRAY

Spend some time praying together before dismissing the group.

Father God, thank You for this precious story that reminds us of Your omniscience and of Your tender care for Your servant, Hannah. Thank You for hearing our prayers, even the ones we can't voice. Even when Your timing doesn't match what we hope or long for, help us surrender our pain to Your all-knowing care. In Jesus' name, we pray, amen.

HOMEWORK

Set aside time this week to work through the personal study on the following pages. The personal study will unpack themes from today's teaching and help you delve deeper into God's Word. Do as much as you can to get the full benefit!

SESSION FOUR

God Hears Your Cries

PERSONAL STUDY

SESSION FOUR OBJECTIVES:

- Explore what God's Word says about His omniscience.
- Read the story of Hannah and look for evidence of God's omniscience.
- See the faithfulness of God on display in the way He knows His children.
- Think about what it looks like to surrender our pain as a response to God's faithfulness.

This week's study draws on themes from chapter 3 of *Now and Not Yet*.

Day 1 | God Is Omniscient

Before you begin today's study, take a moment to quiet your mind and pray. Ask God to teach you from His Word, and ask the Holy Spirit to help you apply that truth to your life.

The narrator of a good story.

Your parents from your perspective of a three-year-old.

The reigning trivia king or queen in your friend group.

Your grandparents when you're in your early thirties.

What do they all have in common?

They know *everything*!

Or at least it seems like they do! Don't you wish you *could* know everything? I think there's something inside all of us that longs to know everything there is to know. Whether it's facts about a specific topic—what it takes to succeed at our jobs, failproof parenting, financial success, the outcome of any given relationship—or just the ability to know *enough*. We long to see what's down the road so we know what we can expect. In short, we long to be omniscient.

But, as we'll learn this week, only God is omniscient, and that is such good news. In fact, it means freedom for us. Freedom to live in the present. Freedom to rest entirely in God's care. Freedom to pour out our hearts to an all-knowing God. Freedom to surrender our pain.

> *God's omniscience means that he fully knows himself and all things actual and possible all at once—he is "all-knowing."*[1]

God's all-knowing nature means that he knows *everything*: past, present, and future.

It's a little mind-boggling when we stop to consider what that really means, but it serves to remind us that God is not like us . . . in the very best ways!

Though the word "omniscient" isn't specifically found in the Bible, this attribute of God is clearly seen from beginning to end.

"God isn't merely knowledgeable; he is omniscient—
limitless in his knowing. He knows all things, not because
he has learned them, but because he is their origin."[2]

READ	WHAT IS IT THAT GOD KNOWS ABOUT?
Psalm 147:5	
1 Chronicles 28:9	
Isaiah 40:28	
Romans 11:33–36	
1 John 3:20	
1 Samuel 10:2	
Acts 2:22, 4:27–28	

DIGGING DEEPER

Let's investigate what God's Word tells us about his omniscience. Read each passage and write down any observations you make about this characteristic of God.

Based on what you observed, what adjectives would you use to describe the omniscience of God?

God's omniscience, paired with His goodness, is a gift! Friend, if you wrestle with feeling unseen and unknown, rest in this truth: God knows you!

GETTING PERSONAL

How does the fact of God's omniscience make you feel? Circle (or write in) all that apply.

SECURE   ANXIOUS   FEARFUL   COMFORTED   CONFUSED   OTHER:_____

Why did you choose the descriptions above?

Is there ever a reason to hide your thoughts or actions from the Lord?[3]

Why is your answer to the above question a blessing in your life?

How might meditating on God's omniscience help you fight against secret sin?

CLOSING PRAYER

Lord God, thank You that You know all things: past, present, and future. Your knowledge is unlimited, perfect, and absolute! Thank You that Jesus made a way for us to come into Your presence fully known, fully loved, and without fear. Help us lean into Your omniscience with joyful hearts. In Jesus' name, we pray, amen.

Day 2 | Hannah's Story:
When Waiting Hurts

Before you begin today's study, take a moment to quiet your mind and pray. Ask God to teach you from His Word, and ask the Holy Spirit to help you apply that truth to your life.

STUDY TIP

Remember, the second day of each week's study is designed to help you see a big-picture story of one person's life. In order to get a big picture, we'll primarily be reading (a lot!) of Scripture and making observations. This context is what we'll draw on for the rest of the week, so take your time and feel free to split up today's study over more than one day if that serves you well.

Today, we're reading Hannah's story, and you'll be happy to hear that our study is contained in a chapter and a half instead of multiple chapters spanning several books! As a heads-up, today's passage involves infertility. If infertility is part of your not-yet-wonderful season, know that I'm praying for you—asking God to meet you in a unique way through our exploration of Hannah's story.

1. Provoked

Read 1 Samuel 1:1–8. What do we learn about Hannah in verse 2?

What's the "cause" of her barrenness as described in verses 5 and 6?

Summarize Hannah's relationship with Peninnah.

DIG DEEPER
Other women who
navigated barrenness:
Sarah
Rebekah
Rachel
The Shunammite Woman
Elizabeth

Describe Elkanah's response to Hannah's barrenness.

2. A Desperate Prayer

Read 1 Samuel 1:9–16. Where does Hannah go to pray?

How does verse 10 describe her prayers?

What vow does Hannah make to the Lord?

What assumption does Eli, the priest, make about Hannah?

Why does he make this assumption (see verse 13)?

Before we move on from Hannah's prayer, I want you to make sure you see her belief in God's omniscience. Did you catch it?

3. Surrender

Read 1 Samuel 1:17–18. Once Hannah explains herself to Eli, what does he do?

How does verse 18 describe Hannah's response to Eli?

How is the way she left the Temple different from the way she entered the Temple?

4. The Birth of Samuel

Read 1 Samuel 1:19–20. How does verse 19 describe God's action on Hannah's behalf?

When does Hannah have Samuel? (How does verse 20 begin?)

5. Keeping Her Vow

Read 1 Samuel 1:21–28. Summarize this passage in a few sentences.

6. A Joyful Prayer

Read 1 Samuel 2:1–11. How does Hannah refer to God in verse 3?

How would you characterize the posture of Hannah's heart based on this prayer?

I hope Hannah's story has been an encouragement to you today, friend. One last question before we reflect on some personal connections to the text:

How would you summarize Hannah's not-yet circumstance?

GETTING PERSONAL

What, if any, pieces of Hannah's story resonate with your own story?

What desperate prayers are you praying in your current season? If you're not personally praying, are there any desperate prayers being prayed by people in your community?

If you had to rate your confidence from 1 (very skeptical) to 5 (totally confident) in the truth that God hears your prayers right now, what would you choose?

1	2	3	4	5

Why did you choose that rating?

CLOSING PRAYER

Jesus, thank You for Hannah's example of what it looks like to pour out our hearts before You, returning again and again, even year after year, to ask You to move! Thank You for her faith and thank You for giving us a peek into her heart. We have a desperate need for You, too, Lord. Help us bring our honest requests and emotions to You, acknowledging that You know all things. It's in Your name we pray, amen.

Day 3 | God's Faithfulness on Display: He Knows *You*

Earlier this week we investigated and observed God's omniscience in several different verses and passages. Remember, God's omniscience means that He knows everything—past, present, and future. We saw this attribute clearly in Hannah's story, too. God was the One who closed her womb, and He knew that, one day, He'd open it. He heard her silent prayers, and He remembered her.

Are there any areas of your life that you feel like God has overlooked or forgotten? What makes you feel that way?

Friend, you're not alone! We've likely all felt that way at some point. Even when we *know* that God sees us, it doesn't always feel like it. When our heads and hearts are out of sync, the best thing we can do is rehearse what's true.

So, today we're going to dig into what may be a familiar passage, to **see and savor** the personal nature of God's omniscience.

PSALM 139

This psalm is written by David, likely around the time that he was made king over all of Israel (in 1048 A.D.).[1] In case you're unfamiliar with David's life, let me tell you—it's yet another now-and-not-yet story in the Bible! David was anointed by Samuel (yes, Hannah's son, Samuel!) as a young boy because God chose him as king for His people. But King Saul (who was reigning at the time) wasn't exactly eager to leave the throne.

**DAVID'S JOURNEY
TO THE THRONE:**

15 years old: Anointed
king by Samuel
(1 Samuel 16:1-13)

30 years old: Installed
as king of Judah
(2 Samuel 5:1-5)

37 years old: Installed
as king over all of Israel
(1 Chronicles 13:4-8)

After many years and a lot of plot twists (including hiding from Saul and running for his life on multiple occasions), David assumes the throne over all of Israel in 1 Chronicles 13:4–8. It's been more than twenty years since Samuel proclaimed God's choice of David, but the promise finally comes to fruition!

It's in this context that Psalm 139 is likely written. Keep the context in mind as you read today!

Read Psalm 139:1–18.

Read it a **second** time, this time out loud.

Now, let's make some observations together. What does David say God knows about him in verses 1–6?

Read Psalm 56:8–11. The word "know" in Psalm 139:2 is the same word that's translated as "kept count of" in Psalm 56:8. What additional context does this provide for Psalm 139?

What is David's response to God's omniscience in verse 6?

Reflecting on Psalm 139:6, Charles Spurgeon paraphrased it this way:

> *"I cannot grasp it. I can hardly endure to think of it. The theme overwhelms me. I am amazed and astounded at it. Such knowledge not only surpasses my comprehension, but even my imagination."[2]*

How does David describe God's presence in verses 7–12?

Read Jeremiah 23:23–24. What additional context does this provide for Psalm 139?

What do verses 13–16 tell us that God knows about David?

Read Psalm 22:9–10 and Psalm 71:6. What additional context do these verses provide for Psalm 139?

One thing is clear after reading this psalm, right? God *knows* David!

God knows all about him—where he is and where he is going. What he's thinking and what he will say. God's presence follows David wherever he goes—he cannot escape it. God knows David from the inside out because He created him—knit him together in his mother's womb!

How would you summarize David's response to God's knowledge in verses 17–18? Does understanding God's omniscience over his life make him joyful? Fearful? Something else?

MORE FAITHFUL THAN YOU KNOW: HE KNOWS *YOU*

Friend, if there's one thing I want you to take away from today, it's this: God knows *you*.

Yes, His omniscience means that His knowledge is infinite and absolute . . . it's big! But it's also personal.

He *made* you. He knows everything about *you*. About *your* life. About what *has* happened, what *is currently* happening, and what *will* happen.

> *". . . in the eternal scheme of things, we cannot lose, because He is a God who can be completely trusted. If we will let Him, God will fill in the details of our lives with His incomparable wisdom and sovereignty plan, written in the indelible ink of His covenant faithfulness and love."[3]*

He sees *you* today, right where you are. He knows *your* not-yet-wonderful circumstances and He knows how you long to be on the other side of it. He loves you!

How does seeing and savoring the personal nature of God's omniscience affect your view of His faithfulness?

He really is more faithful than we know!

GETTING PERSONAL

What emotions does the personal nature of God's omniscience elicit for you? Why?

In what ways might acknowledging God's omniscience change the way you approach prayer?

Try writing your own version of a portion of Psalm 139 on the following page. (Don't worry, you don't have to share it with anyone unless you want to—this is just for your own meditation and application of God's Word!)

1. Write 1–3 sentences describing the ways God knows your thoughts and day-to-day movements.

2. Write 1–3 sentences describing the presence of God in your life.

3. Write 1–3 sentences describing God as the Creator of your physical life.

4. Write 2–3 sentences praising God for His omniscience.

CLOSING PRAYER

God, You made us, You know us, and You're always with us—what more could we ask for? Thank You for Psalm 139 and for how it reminds us of what is true: that You are personally acquainted with all of our ways, that we cannot escape Your presence, and that we have been created by Your hand on purpose and for a purpose. May remembering Your omniscience change the way we pray and the way we wait. In Jesus' name, we pray, amen.

Day 4 | Surrender Your Pain

When I think about the pain that Hannah must have felt—being provoked year by year, bearing the weight of cultural expectations, and feeling shame because of her childless existence—I can't help but feel overwhelmed and think about my own experiences of deep pain.

There are lots of paths pain can tempt us to walk down, and many of them are unhealthy and unhelpful . . . but there's at least one path available to us that leads to life and bears fruit we can't even imagine: the path of surrender.

Far too often, we want to control the situation—to force it into something "manageable," at least from our human perspective. When the pain of a given circumstance threatens to take us out, we'd rather "fix" it than endure the pain.

Even when we stop and remember that God is omniscient, which should help us trust His will, His Word, and His timing, surrendering to that will, Word, and timing isn't easy. And yet, that's the example we see in the life of Hannah.

Let's take a closer look at what "surrender" means . . . and *doesn't* mean.

THE FRUIT OF SURRENDER

Merriam-Webster defines surrender this way: to yield to the power, control, or possession of another upon compulsion or demand.[1] The Bible doesn't explicitly use the word "surrender" when it talks about our posture before God, but it does have a lot to say about humility, following God's direction, and submitting to His will.

Read each of the passages on the following page and answer the questions to complete the table.

Based on what you read, briefly summarize an answer to both questions:

READ	WHAT DOES SURRENDER, HUMILITY, OR SUBMITTING "LOOK LIKE"?	WHAT'S THE BENEFIT OR FRUIT?
James 4:8–10		
Proverbs 3:5–6		
Romans 12:1–2		
Galatians 2:20		
Mark 14:34–36		
1 Peter 5:6		
Hebrews 4:16		

What does surrender, humility, or submission "look like"?

What's the benefit of that posture?

In your opinion, are the benefits worth the surrender or humility required? Why or why not?

WHAT SURRENDER DOESN'T MEAN

I want to make sure we see surrender for what it is—an appropriate response to the omniscience of God—and what it isn't—a fast-track way to get what you desire.

This is not a name-it-and-claim-it approach to God's will . . . that as soon as you surrender your pain and stop trying to control the situation, God will give you what you want. Surrender is about your heart posture more than it is the result.

When you surrender the pain of your not-yet-wonderful circumstance, you are submitting to the omniscience of God. Your posture before Him is one of humility . . . and *that's* the "win." That humility is what will change the way you experience waiting in any now-and-not-yet season.

Even if God doesn't answer your prayer the way you hoped, you can rest in the knowledge that He knows . . . He's trustworthy . . . and He's faithful. Friend, He has not overlooked you or forgotten you.

GETTING PERSONAL

I want us to return to some of the questions you discussed in your group time after the teaching video for this week's study. You may have answered them already, but even if you did, I'd like you to revisit them. It's okay if nothing has changed, but I'm praying you have some additional insight after studying Hannah's story and taking a closer look at Psalm 139.

How would you describe your current posture before the Lord? Would you say it leans more toward surrender or more toward clenched fists when it comes to your not-yet circumstance?

What is it that you're most tempted to control in your current circumstance or season of life?

What do you think surrendering your pain or desire for control would entail?

What's your biggest obstacle to surrender?

Father God, thank You for an omniscience that is personal. Thank You that You know us individually. You made us and You see us, and You know everything that has ever happened, is happening right now, and will happen in the future. Help us submit to Your omniscience and surrender our pain and any desire we have to control the situation. You are the only One who knows all things. And You love us. You are faithful. Remind us, Lord! In Jesus' name, we pray, amen.

Day 5 | Reflection

Reflection is a powerful tool for internalizing the things we've learned about God, about how He works, and about ourselves. Begin today by praying and asking God to show you how this week's study specifically applies to your now-and-not-yet life.

I do not doubt that this week has been intense for some of you as you wrestle with your own pain and what it means to surrender it to the Lord. Hang in there, friend. Keep pressing in.

Take some time to read through your observations and insights in Days 1–4 of this week's study.

What are your top three takeaways from this week?

What truth(s) can you preach to yourself based on this week's study? (List as many things as you can. You may not need to preach all these truths to yourself in your current season, but you never know when they *will* be needed.)

Based on this week's study, complete this sentence:

God is more faithful than I know because _____.

What is one small, tangible step you can take *in the coming week* to surrender your pain? It may be as simple as talking openly and honestly to God about your pain or choosing a verse to memorize. Don't let this week of study pass by without making a practical "resolution" for pressing in. If nothing comes to mind, write a prayer asking God to direct you to take one small step.

CLOSING PRAYER

A Liturgy for When You Feel Invisible
From *Now and Not Yet*

*In a world that's clamoring to be seen,
to be known, and to be loved by all,
there is no end of ways I can make myself
bigger, louder, or more recognizable.
Lord, I confess it feels appealing to be
more acknowledged, more appreciated, more wanted.
But You, God, created me for Yourself,
for me to know You and be known by You,
to be a bearer of Your image.
Not for platforms or stages, applause, or praises.
I was made in secret,
but You formed me and know me intimately.
While the world looks to appearances, achievements,
and accolades,
You look at the heart.
My efforts may be overlooked by others,
but You are El-Roi,
the God who sees me.
The real me.
The messy me.
The me I don't always like.
You tell me I am seen, known, and loved by You.
To hide beneath the shelter of Your wings
is not obscurity but security.
Hidden doesn't mean forgotten,
because You are the God who knows all and sees
everything.
"Rock of Ages, cleft for me, let me hide myself in Thee."
Amen.*

God's Sufficiency Meets Your Weakness

GROUP SESSION

OPENING

Have a volunteer read the opening out loud for the group.

"When I look at Scripture, it's clear that capability is about calling more than giftedness."[1]

In general, our society celebrates giftedness above all else. *Look at what she can do! Her skills are off the chart! She's worked so hard to get where she is!* Culturally, we hardly give a second thought to the idea of a calling because we're so focused on whether we have what it takes to succeed, achieve, or get ahead.

In fact, if we don't feel like we have the necessary skills, there's a good chance we'll skip the task altogether. We'd rather not try at all than try and shine a spotlight on an area of weakness.

And yet, as we'll discover in the coming week, in God's economy, weakness is an opportunity . . . because God's callings are His enablings.

SCRIPTURE: 2 CORINTHIANS 12:5-10

Open your Bibles and have a volunteer read this week's Scripture out loud for the group. It doesn't matter which translation you have—reading God's Word together is always a good idea!

WARM-UP QUESTION

Take a few moments to think about the question individually before asking for one or two volunteers to share their answers with the group.

What's an area of life you tend to feel weak in? Why?

WATCH THE SESSION FIVE VIDEO

Scripture referenced in this session: Romans 8:24-28; Acts 9:20; 2 Corinthians 11:24-29; 2 Corinthians 12:7-9; Philippians 1:18-21

Feel free to use this space to take notes.

GROUP DISCUSSION QUESTIONS

Use the following questions to help process the themes from the video session. You may not get to every question and that's okay!

1. What weakness or insufficiency are you currently facing?

2. In what areas do you see glimpses of *God's* sufficiency in your life?

3. How are you currently (or have you in the past) experiencing the power of God? (Think of ways in your life, in your church, and in any other areas.)

4. What habits, practices, or rhythms might help you consistently shift your focus to God's character instead of your discomfort or pain?

5. Are you letting your not-yet circumstance drive you to prayer? Why or why not?

PRAY

Spend some time praying together before dismissing the group.

Lord, we confess today that we are weak in ways we'll never be able to account for, and that the only remedy is to rest in the sufficiency of Your grace. As we navigate today's not-yet circumstances, may we experience freedom as we embrace our weaknesses and turn to Your unending supply of power. May Your power in our weaknesses show Christ to others. It's in His name we pray, amen.

HOMEWORK

Set aside time this week to work through the personal study on the following pages. The personal study will unpack themes from today's teaching and help you delve deeper into God's Word. Do as much as you can to get the full benefit!

God's Sufficiency Meets Your Weakness

PERSONAL STUDY

SESSION FIVE OBJECTIVES:

- Understand what it means that God is omnipotent.
- Explore the life of Paul and see God's power as the source of his ministry.
- See God's faithfulness on display in the way He gives His all-sufficient power to His people.
- Respond to God's faithfulness by reflecting on what it means to embrace our weaknesses as an opportunity to see and experience God's power.

This week's study draws on themes from chapters 7 and 9 of *Now and Not Yet*.

Day 1 | God Is Omnipotent

Before you begin today's study, take a moment to quiet your mind and pray. Ask God to teach you from His Word and ask the Holy Spirit to help you apply that truth to your life.

Think back to our first week of Bible study together. Do you remember how Sarah responded to God's promise that she would indeed have a baby in her old age? She laughed, thinking there was absolutely no way it was possible.

Did you notice God's response to her laughter? In Genesis 18:14, He says: "Is anything too hard for the LORD?" This rhetorical question, asked by an omnipotent God, helps frame today's study . . . *is* anything too hard for Him?

God's omnipotence means that He is all-powerful. As Bible teacher Jen Wilkin describes it:

"He is not merely possessed of great power, he is all-powerful, limitless in power, infinitely powerful . . . Because God is not bound by location or time, his power is able to be exercised anywhere, any time."[1]

DIGGING DEEPER

Let's look at how the Bible talks about God's power. Read each verse or passage and write down any observations you make. Here are a few questions to keep in mind as you read:

- Who or what does God have power over?
- What is His power compared to?
- Who does He give power to?
- What does His power accomplish?

READ	OBSERVATIONS
2 Chronicles 20:5–6	
Job 42:1–2	
Psalm 29:3–11	
Psalm 115:3	
Isaiah 40:28–29	
Isaiah 45:5–7	
Jeremiah 32:26–27	
Matthew 8:23–27	
Matthew 19:26	
Romans 1:20	

Did anything in these passages surprise you?

Which passage resonated with you most? Why?

Simply *believing* that God is all-powerful isn't a huge stretch for most of us . . . we know Him as Creator, and we see His power in nature on a regular basis. We *know* He's omnipotent, but we don't always *remember* what that actually means.

Based on the passages you read today, how would you describe the connection between God's power and your everyday life?

We'll dig into this connection between God's omnipotence and your daily life later this week, so keep your answer to this question in mind!

Think about a time you witnessed or experienced the power of God. What happened? What was it like? How did it make you feel?

How closely are your belief in God's omnipotence and your actions based on His omnipotence aligned?

What would it take to align your belief and actions more closely?

CLOSING PRAYER

God, all glory and honor and power belong to You! Thank You for all the ways Your Word records Your power for us and for all the ways we've experienced it in our own lives. May remembering Your omnipotence bring us comfort and encouragement in our now-and-not-yet circumstances. In Jesus' name, we pray, amen.

Day 2 | Paul's Story: Persistent Weakness

Before you begin today's study, take a moment to quiet your mind and pray. Ask God to teach you from His Word, and ask the Holy Spirit to help you apply that truth to your life.

STUDY TIP

Remember, the second day of each week's study is designed to help you see a big-picture story of one person's life. In order to get a big picture, we'll primarily be reading (a lot!) of Scripture and making observations. This context is what we'll draw on for the rest of the week, so take your time and feel free to split up today's study over more than one day if that serves you well.

Today we're exploring the theme of God's faithfulness in the context of the life of Paul.

If you've been a follower of Christ for any length of time, chances are you've heard about and read some of Paul's story. Born in Tarsus (modern-day Turkey), Paul was both an Israelite and a Roman citizen, and his primary ministry was to Gentiles (non-Jewish people).

Let's dig into what the Bible tells us about Paul's life and ministry.

1. Pharisee of Pharisees

Read Galatians 1:13–14 and Philippians 3:4–6. How does Paul describe himself?

Read Acts 7:54–8:3. This passage recounts the stoning of Stephen, a follower of Jesus and early church leader. What is Saul's involvement in this narrative?

How would you summarize Saul/Paul's life before Christ?

SAUL OR PAUL?

"Saul" is a Hebrew name, while "Paul" is a Greek name. Contrary to popular belief, there's no evidence to suggest that Saul's name was *changed* to Paul. However, after his missionary journeys began to take him away from Jerusalem (Hebrew people), he is more often referred to by the Greek (or Gentile) name Paul.[1] We'll use both names in this session, depending on what the text refers to him as.

2. The Damascus Road

Read Acts 9:1–19. What is Saul's attitude toward disciples of Christ?

What is his request to the high priest?

Who does he specifically meet on the road to Damascus (see verse 5)?

Summarize his encounter with Jesus.

What role does Ananias play in Saul's conversion to "the Way" (verse 2)?

Paul later recounts the story of his conversion in Acts 22:6–11 and Acts 26:12–18. Do these accounts offer you any additional insight?

3. Planting and Strengthening Churches

DEFINITION

Gospel: It literally means "good news" and refers to the life-changing truth that Jesus' death and resurrection ensure our ability to enjoy a reconciled relationship with God. One pastor[2] summarizes the gospel in four succinct statements:

God is holy.
I am not.
Jesus saves.
Christ is my life.

Read Romans 1:1, Galatians 1:1, and Ephesians 1:1. How does Paul describe himself at the beginning of each of these letters?

Read Galatians 1:15–16. How does Paul describe his calling?

Read Romans 1:14–17. How would you summarize Paul's ministry?

4. Hardship

Read 2 Corinthians 11:24–29. Make a list of the ways Paul suffered.

Read 2 Corinthians 11:30. What does Paul resolve to boast about?

BIBLE FACT
The term Gentile refers to any non-Jewish person.

5. The Thorn

Read 2 Corinthians 12:6–8. How does Paul describe the thorn in his flesh?

DEFINITION
Boast: talk with excessive pride and self-satisfaction about one's achievements, possessions, or abilities.

How many times does he ask God to take it away?

Keep reading 2 Corinthians 12:9–10. How does God respond to Paul's requests?

How does Paul move on?

Thank you for persevering in this exploration of the life of Paul! What you read about and observed today sets the tone for where we'll pick up tomorrow. I know it was a lot, but I'm so grateful you're investing time and energy in reading God's Word with me!

Does any part of Paul's story resonate with your own story? If so, what, and how?

How do you imagine Paul might have felt each time he pleaded with God to remove the thorn in his flesh?

Have you ever felt the same way when asking God for something?

CLOSING PRAYER

Lord Jesus, thank You for the life and ministry and endurance of Paul! Thank You for the record of it in Your Word and for the letters he wrote that instruct and encourage us even now. Holy Spirit, teach us to embrace weakness like Paul did, fully relying on the power of God to equip us. We love You, Jesus, and we ask these things in Your name, amen.

Day 3 | God's Faithfulness on Display: Equipping Power

Before you begin today's study, take a moment to quiet your mind and pray. Ask God to teach you from His Word, and ask the Holy Spirit to help you apply that truth to your life.

Because God is the very definition of all-powerful, you can view nearly every book of the Bible through the lens of His power.

Whether it's His power:

to create the world and everything in it (Genesis),

to lead and protect His people (Exodus),

on display in judgment (the books written by prophets),

to fulfill His promise by sending Jesus (the gospels),

over sin and death (the gospels),

given to believers through the Holy Spirit (Acts),

or His power to reign victorious forever (Revelation),

the power of God is on full display in His Word from beginning to end.

And the truly stunning reality is that all of creation is utterly dependent on God's power and willingness to *equip* humanity with what they need. Our all-powerful God gives us access to His power for our *daily* life.

We heard testimony of this truth in the way Paul talked about his ministry at just about every stage. He was constantly pointing to the power of God (rather than his own ability or power) as the source of his ministry.

Let's take a closer look:

Read Ephesians 3:1–7. What does Paul point to as the origin of his ministry (verse 7)?

Paul knew the power of God firsthand, and he wanted those he shepherded to know that same power. Let's look at a couple of examples:

FOR THE EPHESIANS

Read Ephesians 3:14–19 and read the prayer Paul prays for the Ephesian church.

Note what he specifically asks for on their behalf in verse 16. Fill in the blanks:

". . . that according to the riches of his glory he may grant you to be _____ with _____ through his _____ in your inner being."

What does the power through His Spirit enable the believers to be able to do (verses 17–19)?

That's quite a list, isn't it?

Out of the following, where do you find yourself in need? Underline as many as are applicable.

- For Christ to dwell in your heart through faith
- That you'd be rooted and grounded in love
- That you have the strength to comprehend the love of God
- That you'd be filled up with all the fullness of God

What's your biggest obstacle to the ones you underlined?

Friend, here's the good news. Whatever you need, God's power can do it! In fact, His power can do even more! Look at how Paul ends the prayer in verses 20–21.

. . . *Far more abundantly* than all that we ask or think . . . according to the POWER at work within us.

What power? The power Paul just asked for in verse 16: the power from the Holy Spirit!

FOR TIMOTHY

Read 1 Timothy 1:3–9. Summarize Paul's thoughts related to the power of God in Timothy's life.

MORE FAITHFUL THAN YOU KNOW: ALL THINGS

Paul isn't the only New Testament writer who points to God's equipping power for believers.

Read 2 Peter 1:3–4. What does the power of God grant us?

What kinds of things come to mind when you hear "life and godliness"?

Can you think of anything that falls outside of those two broad categories?

Oh, friend! I hope today's study has been a tangible encouragement to your soul as you've seen that God's omnipotence will meet our need for empowerment. He really is more faithful than we know!

GETTING PERSONAL

In what ways has your perspective on the power of God changed after today's study?

How might rehearsing the truth of God's power granted to you change the way you pray about your not-yet circumstances?

What things pertaining to "life and godliness" do you need from the Lord today?

CLOSING PRAYER

Use the following prompt as a springboard for your own personal prayer:

Jesus, You are so faithful! Your power is . . .

Thank You for all the ways Your power has equipped me to . . .

As I navigate my way through not-yet-wonderful seasons and circumstances, help me remember . . .

In Jesus' name, I pray, amen.

Day 4 | Embracing Weakness

Before you begin today's study, take a moment to quiet your mind and pray. Ask God to teach you from His Word, and ask the Holy Spirit to help you apply that truth to your life.

If you're someone who studies the table of contents before you dive into a study, did today's title catch your eye? If so, did you scoff? Cringe just a little bit? If you did, you're probably not the only one. Embracing weakness isn't something that feels immediately appealing—or maybe even remotely possible—but hang in there with me today. Let's unpack it together.

Remember where we left off in our exploration of Paul's story? Turn back to 2 Corinthians 12:9–10. How does Paul describe his thorn in verses 9–10?

Think about a time when you felt weak, whether physically, emotionally, mentally, or spiritually. Take a moment to briefly describe the situation or circumstances.

Which of the following best describes your natural inclination when you're faced with personal weakness?

DENY   AVOID   SELF-DEPRECATION

IGNORE   ANGER   OTHER: _____

HIDE   SARCASM

Read verses 9 and 10 again. What is Paul's response?

He **embraces** his weakness . . . he resolves to boast about it. And not just any boasting. *Glad* boasting!
Why?

(verse 9b) ". . . so that _____."

Paul's decision to boast about his weakness is anchored in a very specific purpose: to experience the power of God at work in and through him.

He embraces *weakness* in order to experience *power*—the power of God Himself!

It seems counterintuitive, but it's a connection we see Paul talk about repeatedly in his letters to the churches.

Read each verse or passage and write down what you observe.

READ	WHO OR WHAT IS WEAK	WHO OR WHAT IS STRONG	FOR WHAT PURPOSE
1 Corinthians 1:17–18, 27–29			
1 Corinthians 2:1–5			
2 Corinthians 4:7–10			

How would you summarize Paul's attitude toward weakness?

For Paul, weakness is an opportunity to be embraced.

Why? Because weakness is an opportunity to see and experience the power of God firsthand.

"In the kingdom of God, weakness is a superpower."[1]

God didn't discard Paul's weakness; He used it. He used it to turn Paul's attention to God's power.

GETTING PERSONAL

In what areas of life do you feel weak or unable to accomplish a task God has given you?

What do you wish were different:

> about yourself?

> about the task?

> about the circumstances?

How might meditating on the power of God change your response to weakness?

Lord, You know my heart and my wrestling. You know all the ways that we feel unable to accomplish the tasks or fulfill Your purposes. You know all our worries and all the reasons we can't do it. And yet, You are a faithful God who promises to meet us in weakness! Teach us to embrace weakness as an opportunity and help us turn our faces to You—confident, hopeful, and expectant—because of Your omnipotence. In Jesus' name, amen.

Day 5 | Reflection

Reflection is a powerful tool for internalizing the things we've learned about God, about how He works, and about ourselves. Begin today by praying and asking God to show you how this week's study specifically applies to your now-and-not-yet life.

Take some time to read through your observations and insights in Days 1–4 of this week's study. What are your top three takeaways from this week?

What truth(s) can you preach to yourself based on this week's study? (List as many things as you can. You may not need to preach all these truths to yourself in your current season, but you never know when they *will* be needed.)

Based on this week's study, complete this sentence:

God is more faithful than I know because _____.

ONE SMALL THING

What is one small, tangible step you can take *in the coming week* to embrace weakness and rejoice? It may be as simple as naming the weakness you're fighting against or sharing your struggles with a godly friend, mentor, or pastor. Don't let this week of study pass by without making a practical "resolution" for pressing in. If nothing comes to mind, write a prayer asking God to direct you to take one small step.

A Liturgy for When Your Feelings Try to Boss You Around
From *Now and Not Yet*

O God, You know my thoughts,
my inner dialogue,
the accurate
and inaccurate stories I tell myself.
And I confess: Your Word is infinitely more true
than the stories I so often rehearse.
When I think weakness is limiting,
may I remember that You call weaknesses
Christ-exalting.
When I consider suffering debilitating,
may I remember that You call suffering refining.
When I see temptations as discouraging,
may I remember that You call temptations defining.
When I believe trials will break me,
may I remember that You call trials sanctifying.
So help me to flip the narrative about hard seasons.
Give me Your words, Your insight, Your point of view.
Take my less-than
narratives
and rewrite them for Yourself.
Equip my mind,
steer my tongue,
soften my heart,
so that the words of my mouth
and meditation of my heart
may be pleasing to You, O God.
Amen.

God's Sanctifying Work Is Sure

GROUP SESSION

OPENING

Have a volunteer read the opening out loud for the group.

We've spent lots of time identifying and celebrating the faithfulness of God in various biblical narratives over the last several weeks, but this week we'll look at our own stories.

- How is it that God is making us more like Himself? And why?
- How is He pursuing us?
- What are the bigger-picture now-and-not-yet pieces of walking with Jesus?
- And what's our role in the whole process?

May this week's session serve to point you to God's faithfulness in your everyday life!

SCRIPTURE: ROMANS 8:28–29

Open your Bibles and have a volunteer read this week's Scripture out loud for the group. It doesn't matter which translation you have—reading God's Word together is always a good idea!

WARM-UP QUESTION

Take a few moments to think about the question individually before asking for one or two volunteers to share their answers with the group.

What comes to mind when you think about the holiness of God? What emotions does it elicit?

WATCH THE SESSION SIX VIDEO

Scripture referenced in this session: 1 John 3:2; Romans 8:28–29; 1 Peter 1:3–9, 13–16; Hebrews 12:1–2; Philippians 1:6; Jude 24–25

Feel free to use this space to take notes.

GROUP DISCUSSION QUESTIONS

Use the following questions to help process the themes from the video session. You may not get to every question and that's okay!

1. Would you say you have a true desire to be holy like God? If not, what holds you back? If so, what helps cultivate that desire?

2. Where do you see evidence of God's sanctifying work in your life, either now or in the past?

3. What habits, practices, or rhythms might help you cultivate a perspective that sees your not-yet circumstances as "light and momentary"?

4. In what ways, if any, do you sense God is asking you to respond or act in the midst of your not-yet-wonderful season?

5. In what ways can you start where you are right now?

PRAY

Spend some time praying together before dismissing the group.

Father, thank You for the reminder in this session that You are after our hearts and that You will not waste any circumstance but will use every piece of our stories—every tension we feel between now and not yet—to make us like Jesus. Change our desires and help us long for holiness, Lord, both for Your glory and for our good. Even as we approach our last week of study, help us to keep learning, keep practicing, and keep applying the truth of Your Word to our lives. We're so grateful for all You have done and are doing. In Jesus' name, we pray, amen.

HOMEWORK

Set aside time this week to work through the personal study on the following pages. The personal study will unpack themes from today's teaching and help you delve deeper into God's Word. Do as much as you can to get the full benefit!

God's Sanctifying Work Is Sure

PERSONAL STUDY

SESSION SIX OBJECTIVES:

- Gain a deeper understanding of what the holiness of God means.
- Explore the already-and-not-yet framework in play for followers of Jesus.
- See God's faithfulness on display in His commitment to your sanctification.
- Reflect on how we can respond to God's faithfulness by starting where we are right now.

This week's study draws on themes from chapter 10 of *Now and Not Yet*.

Day 1 | God Is Holy

Before you begin today's study, take a moment to quiet your mind and pray. Ask God to teach you from His Word, and ask the Holy Spirit to help you apply that truth to your life.

God's holiness means that He is separated from sin and devoted to seeking His own honor.[1] In every way, He is pure and set apart, and His desire is that we would set ourselves apart for Him.[2]

Thousands of pages, written by far more knowledgeable theologians than I, have been written about the holiness of God and what it means for Christ-followers to pursue holiness. It's a huge topic and one where we'll only scratch the surface in our study today, but my prayer is that our quick overview helps set a foundational framework for you!

DEFINING HOLINESS

The Hebrew word for *holy* means apartness, holiness, sacredness, or separateness.[3] The Hebrew root word that the noun comes from means to consecrate, sanctify, prepare, dedicate, be hallowed, be holy, be sanctified, or be separate. [4]

Let's revisit the First Mention Principle we utilized in week 3 to see what kind of insight we can gain about the word *holy*.

The first time we see the noun form is in Exodus 3:5 when God appears to Moses in the burning bush:

> "Then [God] said, "Do not come near; take your sandals off your feet, for the place on which you are standing is *holy* ground" (emphasis added).

RECOMMENDED
ONLINE BIBLE
STUDY RESOURCES
Whether you're looking
for a different translation,
a commentary,
background information,
or information about
the original word,
check out these free
online resources:

BlueLetterBible.org
BibleGateway.com
BibleStudyTools.com

The first time we see the root word is even earlier, in Genesis 2:3:

"So God blessed the seventh day and made it *holy*, because on it God rested from all his work that he had done in creation" (emphasis added).

Use an online Bible study site to read these verses in a few different versions. How else is "holy" translated?

Based on the other translations you read, and the heart behind the First Mention Principle, how would you summarize the concept of holiness in your own words?

DIGGING DEEPER

Let's look at some other passages that talk about the holiness of God.

Read each verse or passage and write down any observations you make about the holiness of God—what it means, what it requires, what response it generates, etc.

Based on your observations, what do you think an appropriate response to the holiness of God entails?

READ	OBSERVATIONS ABOUT GOD'S HOLINESS
Exodus 15:11	
Leviticus 11:44–45	
1 Samuel 2:2	
Psalm 96:7–9	
Isaiah 6:1–5	
1 Peter 1:14–16	
Revelation 15:2–4	

SO WHAT?

At this point in today's study, I hope you're asking yourself this very important question: So what?! Why does it matter that God is holy?

R. C. Sproul explained it this way:

> *"Holiness is the characteristic of God's nature*
> *that is at the very core of His being. Only as*
> *we encounter God in His holiness is it possible*
> *for us to see ourselves as we really are."*[5]

In order for us to know who God is and understand who we really are, we have to get a grasp on God's holiness. God's holiness is foundational to the *gospel*! And, as we'll explore later this week, foundational to being made more like Jesus.

GETTING PERSONAL

What, if anything, surprised you in today's study?

How close is your response to the holiness of God to the responses you observed in Scripture today?

What factors do you think contribute to a disconnect between the response to God's holiness we read about in the Word and our own responses?

What habits, practices, or rhythms would help you cultivate an appropriate response to God's holiness?

CLOSING PRAYER

Use the following prayer prompt as a springboard for your own personal prayer:

Father God, You are holy! Thank You for Your holiness because . . .

Thank You for making a way for me to be made holy through Jesus. I am so grateful for . . .

Help me, by Your Spirit, to keep growing in holiness as I . . .

In Jesus' name, I pray, amen.

Day 2 | Your Story

Before you begin today's study, take a moment to quiet your mind and pray. Ask God to teach you from His Word, and ask the Holy Spirit to help you apply that truth to your life.

So far in our study, day 2 has been the day we read about a biblical character (or nation!) to get some context for how the faithfulness of God is on display. However, in this last week, I want to take a look at our own stories and unpack the theological framework that all of our now-and-not-yet conversations are based on.

NOW AND NOT YET

If you're anything like me, your *right now* may not be anything like what you imagined or hoped it would be. On some level, we're likely all navigating *right now* circumstances that we'd rather skip altogether.

The reality of life's persistent pressures, disappointments, heartaches, unresolved issues, and detours often add up to a distinctly not-yet-wonderful right now . . . and we long for resolution, relief, joy, and ease.

Think about the characters and stories we've explored in the last several weeks. *All* of them faced a not-yet-wonderful reality, right? Flip back through your study to refresh your memory and note what each person's (or nation's) "not yet" was:

CHARACTER	"NOT YET"
Abraham	
Joseph	
The nation of Israel	
Hannah	
Paul	

What about you? What pieces of your current reality are not yet wonderful? What season or circumstance has you longing for relief, resolution, ease, or joy?

If you could change anything about your current situation, reality, or season, what would it be?

Friend, the tension created by the gap between what we want our circumstances to be and how they really are is *real*. But so is the faithfulness of God!

The deeper theological concept undergirding the themes we've looked at so far is what biblical scholars have called the already-but-not-yet or the now-and-not-yet framework.

DEFINITION

Meta-narrative: the "big picture" story of the Bible—God's plans and purposes on display from Genesis to Revelation.

This framework helps followers of Jesus locate themselves in the meta-narrative of Scripture. Why "already but not yet"? Consider it with me. . . . We live in a time after Jesus' life on earth, His death, and His resurrection. That means He has: *already* rescued the world, *but not yet* set up His eternal reign, and *already* come to earth fully God and fully man, *but not yet* returned to gather His people for eternity.

Let's see how the Bible talks about it:

Read 1 John 3:2–3. What does John identify as the current reality for Christ followers?

What does John identify as the "not-yet" reality that is to come?

He's reminding his readers that their present experience of a spiritual reality isn't the whole picture. One day, their physical and spiritual realities will be in sync, but until then, they (us, too!) will live in the tension of already and not yet.

Read each of the following passages and consider what each is saying is *already* true. Then write down the current reality, or *not-yet* reality.

READ	ALREADY	NOT YET
Romans 7:21–25		
1 Corinthians 13:8–12		
Ephesians 4:17–24		
Revelation 21:1–4		

Do any other already-and-not-yet states of being come to mind? If so, write them down.

In what ways does this quick overview of "already and not yet" affect the way you think about the faithfulness of God?

Typically, at the end of day 2, I'd have you summarize the not-yet circumstance of the person or nation we studied that day . . . but today, the question is for you.

What would you say is your most pressing not-yet-wonderful circumstance right now? Is it something physical? Mental? Emotional? Spiritual? Relational?

Know that I'm praying for you in this last week of Bible study, friend. I'm asking "the God of endurance and encouragement" (Romans 15:5) to meet you exactly where you are.

GETTING PERSONAL

What, if any, "already" do you need to meditate on this week?

What, if any, "not yet" do you need to talk to the Lord about this week?

CLOSING PRAYER

Father, thank You for Your Word that teaches us about who You are, who we are, and the nature of our life in Christ. Thank You for every "already" and for your promise to fulfill every "not yet." Truly, every promise is "Yes and Amen" in Christ! Help us rest in faithfulness. In Jesus' name, amen.

Day 3 | God's Faithfulness on Display: Your Sanctification

Before you begin today's study, take a moment to quiet your mind and pray. Ask God to teach you from His Word, and ask the Holy Spirit to help you apply that truth to your life.

If you've ever set the table with the "nice dishes," or done a last-minute load of laundry to have that *one* pair of jeans you love so much ready for an evening out with your girlfriends, you already know, on the most basic level, what it means to "sanctify" something.

To sanctify something means to wash, cleanse, and set it aside for a special purpose.[1]

When we're talking about Christ-followers being sanctified, we mean that they are being purified and set apart for God's use and purposes.[2] In other words, sanctification is the incremental process by which something is *made holy*.

On day 1 of this week, we briefly studied the holiness of God, and the verses we read made it clear that though He is holy, we, by nature, are not. But, when we put our faith in the death and resurrection of Jesus, we are made new.

> "Therefore, if anyone is in Christ, he is a new creation.
> The old has passed away; behold, the new has come."
> 2 Corinthians 5:17

From that point on, for the rest of our lives, we're continually being made more and more like Christ. As we practice putting off our old selves and putting on our new identities, we grow in holiness!

The ESV Study Bible describes sanctification like this:

> *"[Sanctification] involves both a* relational *component (separation from participating in and being influenced by evil) and a* moral *component (growth in holiness or moral purity in attitudes, thoughts, and actions)."[3]*

Based on these descriptions, how would you describe:

Your role in sanctification?

God's role in your sanctification?

Let's see what God's Word has to say about it!

Read each verse or passage and write down what action is happening. Then think about what that means for our role, and what God's role is in the process.

READ	ACTION HAPPENING	ROLES
Philippians 2:12–13		Our role: God's role:
Philippians 3:13–14		Our role: God's role:
Hebrews 12:14		Our role: God's role:
John 15:1–5		Our role: God's role:

Based on what you just read, how would you summarize our role and God's role in sanctification?

How are they different?

MORE FAITHFUL THAN YOU KNOW:
A PROMISE TO COMPLETE

Here's the best news, friend: God wants you to be holy more than you do!

Read Romans 8:29–30 and summarize what Paul is reminding the Romans.

Do you see the progression? It's already been determined that everyone who puts their faith in Jesus will be conformed to His image! God has already said that He will do it!

And, as Romans 8:28 reminds us, He'll work *everything* out toward that purpose. He won't waste anything—any season, any hardship, any joy, any between. Your not-yet-wonderful circumstances are tools in His hands . . . tools that will shave down your sharp edges and form your soul into a pure, set-apart resource useful for God's purposes.

But only *if* you'll submit to Him . . . if you'll believe what He says is true, steward the life you've been given, trust His provision, surrender your pain, and embrace your weakness so that you can start where you are.

Paul was so confident of God's commitment to our sanctification that he wrote about this in Philippians 1:6. Read the verse and write it down:

Paul is *sure*.

Here's how Eugene Peterson paraphrased that verse in The Message:

> "There has never been the slightest doubt in my mind that the God who started this great work in you would keep at it and bring it to a flourishing finish on the very day Christ Jesus appears."[4]
> Philippians 1:6 MSG

Never the slightest doubt.

God *will* make us perfectly holy when Jesus returns to reign forever . . . and until then, we will work out our salvation here on earth. Already promised, not yet realized.

He really is more faithful than we know.

GETTING PERSONAL

If sanctification involves both a relational and moral component, how would you rate yourself on a scale of 1 (not pursuing at all) to 5 (consistently and actively pursuing) for each one? (circle)

RELATIONAL (separation from participating in and being influenced by evil)

1   2   3   4   5

MORAL (growth in holiness or moral purity in attitudes, thoughts, and actions)

1   2   3   4   5

In what ways are you actively pursuing sanctification?

Are there any habits, practices, or rhythms you need to establish to take a more active role?

What verse or verses would be helpful for you to memorize from this week?

CLOSING PRAYER

Lord, You are so faithful! You save us and You form us . . . You're making us more and more like Jesus and You promise to complete the work You've started. We are so grateful! Help us engage with You and with the processes of sanctification— consistently and actively—while also trusting Your Spirit to change us and empower us for the next step. We love You, Lord! In Jesus' name, amen.

Day 4 | Start Where You Are

Before you begin today's study, take a moment to quiet your mind and pray. Ask God to teach you from His Word, and ask the Holy Spirit to help you apply that truth to your life.

It's easy to long for our circumstances to change, for relief and resolution and something easier than *right now,* isn't it? There's nothing wrong with those desires . . . but if we focus on them to the exclusion of making the most of what God has given us right now, those desires can rob us of the joys found in embracing sanctification as a gift from God.

Each week so far, day 4 has been an exploration of a biblical character's example to us . . . but today, I want to encourage you with one simple phrase: *Start where you are.*

You will not finish this study, stand in awe of the faithfulness of God, and then magically operate from a continual place of joy, confidence, and hope in the places that apathy, fear, and lack of vision once occupied. (Don't you wish you could, though?)

Instead, you and I have to keep fighting for joy, confidence, and hope. We'll have to guard against coasting and growing complacent. We will have to explore, dig in, and be sure we fully grasp the faithfulness of God on display through Christ.

Read Philippians 2:12–13. What is Paul encouraging believers to do?

Are they to do it alone?

No!

Write out verse 13:

Paul is calling them to persevere, remain steadfast, and keep pressing on in their efforts to walk with God, all the while *knowing that God is faithful.*

John Piper, summarizing a thought from George Mueller, further explains this train of thought:

> *"In other words, labor with all your might, but do not trust in your labor—trust in God. Plan hard, but don't trust in your plans—trust in God. Speak clearly and creatively, but don't trust in your speaking—trust in God. Sing, but don't trust in your singing—trust in God. Create and produce and lead and manage, but don't trust in your creativity and leadership and management and productivity—trust in God."[1]*

Everything in me wants to shout an emphatic "Yes!" to Piper's encouragement . . . but at the same time, something deep inside of me asks, "But, how?" Maybe you do, too?

LIVING IN THE TENSION

The New Testament writers tended to close their encouragements and reminders to fellow believers in the early church with a clear framework for persevering in faith:

- Believe what Jesus said about Himself and those who are in Christ, and

- Respond accordingly.

And there's almost always a keyword repeated as they lay out what the response should be. It's the word "therefore."

In essence, they're saying, "In light of the truth of who God is and what He's done, we *therefore* can and will live differently going forward." The authors' call to action is always followed by the call to believe.

So, as we consider what it means to start where we are, let's look at one of my favorite *therefores*.

Read Hebrews 12:1–2. Make a list of the actions that follow "therefore."

Consider what each "therefore" means for you, *right now* . . . even today.

What would it look like for you to throw off entangling sin?

What would it look like for you to run with perseverance?

What would it look like for you to fix your eyes on Jesus?

Friends, hear my encouragement to you: start where you are! You won't do it perfectly and it won't necessarily come easily, but if it's worth doing at all, it's worth starting now, even if you're not good at it!

GETTING PERSONAL

For the rest of our time together today, I want you to be really honest and get really practical.

What would you start doing today in obedience if you weren't afraid of failure, if you didn't worry about the future, and if you knew that God has you right where you are for a reason?

What's preventing you from starting?

CLOSING PRAYER

Use this prompt as a springboard for personal prayer:

Lord, I confess that I have let _____ distract me from _____. Help me remember _____ and by the power of the Holy Spirit, use that truth to motivate me to start where I am when it comes to _____. In Jesus' name, amen.

Day 5 | Reflection

Reflection is a powerful tool for internalizing the things we've learned about God, about how He works, and about ourselves. Begin today by praying and asking God to show you how this week's study specifically applies to your now-and-not-yet life.

Take some time to read through your observations and insights in Days 1–4 of this week's study. What are your top three takeaways from this week?

What truth(s) can you preach to yourself based on this week's study? (List as many things as you can. You may not need to preach all these truths to yourself in your current season, but you never know when they *will* be needed.)

Based on this week's study, complete this sentence:

God is more faithful than I know because _____.

What is one small, tangible step you can take *in the coming week* to embrace sanctification and start where you are? It may be as simple as writing down a simple action plan or talking about this week's study with a friend. Don't let this week of study pass by without making a practical "resolution" for pressing in. If nothing comes to mind, write a prayer asking God to direct you take to one small step.

CLOSING PRAYER

A Liturgy for When You Don't Know What to Do
From *Now and Not Yet*

Here I stand, with the details of my past,
the not-yets of my present,
and the unknowns of the future You hold.
I'm ready to be shaped and molded by my Maker,
that I might be an instrument of hope,
a vessel of truth, a conduit of grace.
May I not be content merely to believe—to
bask in the redemption that has been
purchased for me—without
consequence or action.
But let me, instead, run the race set before me today,
with the finished work of Christ in view.
Consume me with the desire to run well.
Fuel me with the grace that ignites,
striving with all my might,
but only in all Your strength, O Lord.
Persevering with joy,
because You hold me fast,
let me not grow weary in doing good.
I renounce my vain attempts at building
my own kingdom and remember, instead,
that I was made for Yours.
Make me a builder, O Lord.
Make me a home for gospel hope—no
matter the duration or design.
I choose to begin today.
Help me begin today.
Amen.

Conclusion

I shared my heart with you in the last teaching video for this session, but it bears repeating here, too. If I have one prayer for both of us, it would be that we would not get stuck, wishing we were somewhere else with a whole different set of circumstances, and miss what God is doing right now, even if our ideals, our dreams, our happy endings, our somedays feel so far away.

So this is me, leaning in to tell you:
You're not alone.
You will make it.
This moment matters, and our God doesn't waste a thing.
Therefore, stay awake, stay present, and press in!
Run to Jesus, not the other way.
Get going and make the most of every opportunity!

Don't sit this season out, friend. There's no time to stay stuck in the past or to be on the fence about today. You've been given hard and wonderful tasks only you are gifted enough to do. You're not right where you are on accident. This is not a passive, wait-and-see game plan; it is a hand-to-the-plow-and-trust-God way of life. And He—our God who is faithful yesterday, today, and forever—will complete what He has begun in us. He promised to.

Jude verses 24 and 25 say:

> "Now to him who is able to keep you from stumbling and to present you blameless before the presence of his glory with great joy, to the only God, our Savior, through Jesus Christ our Lord, be glory, majesty, dominion, and authority, before all time and now and forever. Amen."

Start where you are and press in, because God has been and will always be faithful in our now and not yet. I love you; Christ loves you more.

Because of grace,

Ruth

An Invitation

Dear friend,

If you're jumping into this study and feel like an outsider when it comes to understanding God's faithfulness in salvation, welcome. This study is for you, too!

Maybe your faith journey hasn't felt much like the grace of God you're reading about here or in God's Word. Or, maybe you've tasted and seen the grace of God and today is your new beginning to walk in that grace.

The gospel—the good news of Jesus Christ—is simply this: The end of earning His favor.

The end of self-reliance

The end of slavery to sin

The end of condemnation

The end of being "good enough"

A beginning in surrender

A beginning in forgiveness

A beginning in holiness

A beginning in freedom

A beginning in loving Christ more. The love story told from the beginning of time began in the Garden, where Adam and Eve knew no separation from their Creator until they exchanged transparency with their God for sinful pride. God, in His mercy, orchestrated and wooed His people for generations so that they might know the weight of their sin and their need for a Savior.

That Savior was Jesus, who lived a sinless life for thirty-three years on Earth in order to fulfill the will of the Father by dying a criminal's death on the cross to pay the penalty of man's disobedience—the penalty of separation that you and I would suffer if not for the shed blood of Christ.

And so, the invitation and welcome is yours: to come broken, hopeless, and burdened . . . and find peace for your soul.

Because of grace,

Ruth

Notes

Session 1 Personal Study: Day 1

1. *Merriam-Webster Dictionary*, s.v. "promise," https://www.merriam-webster.com/dictionary/promise?utm_campaign=sd&utm_medium=serp&utm_source=jsonld.

2. Wayne Grudem, *Systematic Theology: An Introduction to Biblical Doctrine* (Leicester, Great Britain: Inter-Varsity Press & Grand Rapids: Zondervan Publishing House, 1994), 195.

3. Ruth Chou Simons, *Pilgrim: 25 Ways God's Character Leads Us Onward* (Eugene, OR: Harvest House Publishers, 2023), 163.

4. Victor Knowls, "Promise and Fulfillment: Believing the Promises of God," *Leaven*, 6(3), 4. https://digitalcommons.pepperdine.edu/cgi/viewcontent.cgi?article=1769&context=leaven. Bernis, J. (2022, May 24). How many prophecies did Jesus fulfill? FIRM Israel. https://firmisrael.org/learn/how-many-prophecies-did-jesus-fulfill/.

5. Jonathan Bernis, "How Many Prophecies Did Jesus Fulfill?" FIRM Israel, January 31, 2015, https://firmisrael.org/learn/how-many-prophecies-did-jesus-fulfill/.

6. Knowls, "Promise and Fulfillment."

Session 1 Personal Study: Day 2

1. Notes on Genesis 17:5 (ESV).

Session 1 Personal Study: Day 3

1. Kevin DeYoung, "Understanding Biblical Covenants Is as Easy as 1, 2, 3," Crossway, November 13, 2020, https://www.crossway.org/articles/understanding-biblical-covenants-is-as-easy-as-1-2-3/.

2. Stephen Wellum, "The Story and Message of the Bible," The Gospel Coalition, February 10, 2021, https://www.thegospelcoalition.org/essay/the-story-and-message-of-the-bible/.

3. Jared T. Parker, "Cutting Covenants," BYU Religious Studies Center, https://rsc.byu.edu/gospel-jesus-christ-old-testament/cutting-covenants.

4. Hoffman, B. (2023, January 16). Cutting a covenant. Olive Tree Blog. https://www.olivetree.com/blog/cutting-a-covenant/.

5. John Piper, "Are the Old Testament Promises Made to Us? Isaiah 41:10," Desiring God, https://www.desiringgod.org/labs/are-the-old-testament-promises-made-to-us.

6. Jason Derouchie, "Is Every Promise 'Yes'? Old Testament Promises and the Christian," *Themelios*, The Gospel Coalition, April 13, 2017, https://www.thegospelcoalition.org/themelios/article/is-every-promise-yes-old-testament-promises-and-the-christian/.

Session 1 Personal Study: Day 4

1. Grudem, *Systematic Theology*, 195.

Session 2: God's Sovereignty Directs a Bigger Story

1. Jon Bloom, "Staying Faithful When Things Just Get Worse," Desiring God, October 6, 2023, https://www.desiringgod.org/articles/joseph-staying-faithful-when-things-just-get-worse.

Session 2 Personal Study: Day 1

1. Simons, *Pilgrim*, 145.

2. Jen Wilkin, *None Like Him: 10 Ways God Is Different from Us (and Why That's a Good Thing)* (Wheaton, IL: Crossway, 2016), 141–142.

Session 2 Personal Study: Day 3

1. Madeleine L'Engle, *A Wrinkle in Time* (New York: Yearling, 1999).

Session 2 Personal Study: Day 4

1. *Vine's Expository Dictionary of New Testament Words*, s.v. "steward, stewardship," Blue Letter Bible, https://www.blueletterbible.org/search/Dictionary/viewTopic.cfm?topic=VT0002768.

Session 3 Personal Study: Day 1

1. Simons, *Pilgrim*, 104.

Session 3 Personal Study: Day 4

1. Johnson Oatman Jr., "Count Your Blessings," Hymnology Archive, https://www.hymnologyarchive.com/count-your-blessings.

Session 4 Personal Study: Day 1

1. Grudem, *Systematic Theology*, 190.

2. Wilkin, *None Like Him*, 109.

3. A great question originally posed by Grudem, *Systematic Theology*, 207.

Session 4 Personal Study: Day 3

1. "Probable Occasion When Each Psalm Was Composed," Blue Letter Bible, https://www.blueletterbible.org/study/parallel/paral18.cfm.

2. Charles Haddon Spurgeon, *The Treasury of David, Volume 3* (Peabody, MA: Hendrickson, 1988).

3. Nancy Leigh DeMoss, *Brokenness, Surrender, Holiness: A Revive Our Hearts Trilogy (Revive Our Hearts Series)* (Chicago: Moody Publishers, 2008), 167.

Session 4 Personal Study: Day 4

1. *Merriam-Webster Dictionary*, s.v. "surrender," https://www.merriam-webster.com/dictionary/surrender.

2. Andrew Murray, *Absolute Surrender: The Blessedness of Forsaking All and Following Christ* (Abbotsford, WI: Aneko Press, 2017).

Session 5: God's Sufficiency Meets Your Weakness

1. Ruth Chou Simons, *Now and Not Yet: Pressing in When You're Waiting, Wanting, and Restless for More* (Nashville: Thomas Nelson, 2024), 115.

Session 5 Personal Study: Day 1

1. Wilkin, *None Like Him*, 125.

Session 5 Personal Study: Day 2

1. Greg Lanier, "No, 'Saul the Persecutor' Did Not Become 'Paul the Apostle,'" The Gospel Coalition, October 31, 2017, https://www.thegospelcoalition.org/article/no-saul-the-persecutor-did-not-become-paul-the-apostle/.

2. Mark Vroegop, (sermon, College Park Church, Indianapolis, IN).

Session 5 Personal Study: Day 4

1. Simons, *Now and Not Yet*, 120.

Session 6 Personal Study: Day 1

1. Grudem, *Systematic Theology*, 201.

2. Simons, *Pilgrim*, 197.

3. *Strong's Hebrew Lexicon (KJV)*, Blue Letter Bible, https://www.blueletterbible.org/lexicon/h6944/kjv/wlc/0-1/.

4. *Blue Letter Bible*, s.v. "qāḏaš," https://www.blueletterbible.org/lexicon/h6942/kjv/wlc/0-1/.

5. R. C. Sproul, "The Importance of Holiness" from "The Holiness of God," Ligonier Ministries, https://www.ligonier.org/learn/series/holiness-of-god/the-importance-of-holiness.

Session 6 Personal Study: Day 3

1. "What Is Sanctification and How Does It Work?" Cru, https://www.cru.org/us/en/train-and -grow/spiritual-growth/sanctification.html.

2. "What Is Sanctification?" Grace Theological Seminary, June 17, 2022, https://seminary.grace .edu/what-is-sanctification/.

3. The Message Bible. (2002). Eugene H. Peterson.

Session 6 Personal Study: Day 4

1. John Piper, "Use Means, but Trust in God," Desiring God, February 17, 2004, https://www.desiringgod.org/messages/use-means-but-trust-in-god.

About the Author

Ruth Chou Simons is a *Wall Street Journal* bestselling and award-winning author of several books and Bible studies, including *GraceLaced*, *Beholding and Becoming*, *When Strivings Cease*, and *TruthFilled*. She is an artist, entrepreneur, podcaster, and speaker, using each of these platforms to sow the Word of God into people's hearts. Through social media and her online shoppe at GraceLaced.com, Simons shares her journey of God's grace intersecting daily life with word and art. Ruth and her husband, Troy, are grateful parents to six boys—their greatest adventure.

ALSO AVAILABLE FROM RUTH CHOU SIMONS

Now and Not Yet

Pressing in When You're Waiting, Wanting, and Restless for More

AVAILABLE IN STORES AND ONLINE!

An Imprint of Thomas Nelson

Let go of endless striving and find rest and freedom in Christ.

Ruth Chou Simons calls women to discover how God's profound gift of grace and favor invites them to rest from chasing approval and earning love, and instead discover the freedom of true belonging and worth that doesn't depend on them.

Check out the Book and Companion Bible study for small groups and churches.

NELSON
BOOKS

An Imprint of Thomas Nelson

Harper *Christian*
Resources